Praise for *Rigorous PBL by Design*
by Michael McDowell

Far too many people assume that problem-based learning simply works. It doesn't. It works when specific conditions are right. It works when the experience is designed in a way that builds students' confidence and competence. That is easier said than done, which is why we are so pleased with this book. It guides readers through specific design features that they can use to ensure deep learning, and transfer of that learning, for students. McDowell has solved the problem and is willing to share his findings with others.

Douglas Fisher and Nancy Frey, Department of Educational Leadership
San Diego State University
San Diego, CA

PBL has finally reached the tipping point. As I meet with school superintendents around the country, most of them have already started or know they need to begin full-scale adoption of PBL in their districts. What has been missing is a clear set of next steps to improve PBL practice. *Rigorous PBL by Design* steps into this void and provides much-needed help by busting PBL myths and designing PBL improvements around "clarity," "challenge," and "culture." McDowell gives teachers and education leaders the concrete guidance they need to assure their PBL practices will meet the needs of their 21st century students.

Ken Kay, CEO
Edleader21

A highly practical and informative guide to project-/problem-based learning.

Jo Boaler, Professor and Co-Founder of YouCubed
Stanford University
Stanford, CA

Educators interested in project- and problem-based learning are advised to read this book and heed its message. Michael McDowell highlights a point that can easily be lost in the enthusiasm for PBL—that the focus must always be on targeted learning outcomes. In other words, the project or problem is a vehicle to engage students in meaningful learning, and we must always keep this end in mind.

Jay McTighe, Author and Consultant
Understanding by Design

This book makes me feel challenged and inspired. The author's message served as an invitation, to review my practice . . . . *Rigorous PBL by Design* provided new direction and justification for why I need to improve my practice.

Ernie Rambo, Teacher, Seventh-Grade US History
Walter Johnson Academy of International Studies

There are more than enough matrices and examples throughout the book to d author's points. I particularly appreciate the extended examples provided via book offers varied examples of grade levels and content to help teachers create based on the author's recommendations.

LaQuita Outlaw, Middle Scl
Bay Shore N
B

This is an outstanding resource for educators, providing a practical framework for creating effective and impactful PBL experiences. We are committed to strengthening our PBL practices and we look forward to adding this valuable resource to our professional reference library.

Rachel Bergren, MSc, Director, Education and Guest Experience
The Marine Mammal Center

This is a very important book at this moment. I see the tremendous potential impact of rigorous PBL on student learning. I will definitely purchase copies as we have large numbers of teachers who employ PBL, and this book will provide them with guidance on how to improve their practice.

Tara Taupier, Assistant Superintendent of Educational Services
Tamalpais Union High School District
Larkspur, CA

This practical guide will resonate with teachers looking to ensure that learning is deep and meaningful. The research provided, the tangible steps outlined, and the examples make the case that this approach must be integrated into all schools.

Tom Hierck, Consultant/Author
Hierck Consulting
Gibsons, BC Canada

This book is very thorough in explaining the differences between PBL done more as a project and done with student self-monitoring and transfer of knowledge. The teacher's role at each student's level (surface, deep, and transfer) is explained clearly.

Dana B. Leonard, SPED High School Teacher
Ledford High School
Thomasville, NC

An excellent tool for any educator, administrator, or professional development coach who wants to dive deep into designing an effective and rigorous PBL. This book provides excellent details for the reader and step-by-step instructions on designing as well as implementing a PBL to enhance student cognition.

Tara Howell, Vice Principal and Educational Leader
Junipero Serra High School
San Diego, CA

PBL, done well, helps students to develop the skills needed to be successful in a rapidly changing world. This book offers both a thought-provoking and practical guide for educators looking to transform their classrooms through PBL. McDowell provides critical insights into common PBL pitfalls and identifies key design shifts that can deeply impact student learning. Novice and experienced PBL teachers alike will find this book helpful in improving their practice and delivering on the promise of PBL.

Megan Pacheco, Chief Learning Officer
New Tech Network
Napa, CA

Hattie's research showed that PBL has a low effect size. However, Hattie's intention behind exposing the effect size was not to have teachers throw it out. Rather, he wanted teachers and leaders to use evidence to look at how they do it, and improve on the process. In *Rigorous PBL by Design*, Michael McDowell does exactly that. McDowell provides a practical, step-by-step process using Hattie's research to help teachers improve PBL so it provides the effect on student learning that it should.

Peter DeWitt, EdD
Author/Consultant
Albany, NY

We need a book that focuses directly on student learning rather than a superficial process of teaching PBL. This book gives teachers the practices and procedures to directly support students in transferring their learning. For practitioners, this book makes a whole lot of sense.

Steve Zipkes, Founding Principal
Cedars International Next Generation High School
Austin, TX

This is a must-read for any teacher wanting to understand how to thoughtfully plan, organize, and carry out in his or her own classroom the kinds of problem- and project-based learning (PBL) that will truly enable students to acquire and demonstrate surface, deep, and transfer of content knowledge and skills at the maximum possible levels. During my 24 years in the classroom teaching elementary and secondary students, I regularly engaged learners in what I thought were correctly timed, well-designed PBL experiences that were both "hands-on/minds-on" and authentic. If I'd had this book to reference then, how much greater could those learning experiences have been for my students—and for me! Michael McDowell's thoroughly researched, instructive, and in-depth volume has now become my gold standard for understanding and applying PBL in today's classrooms. *Rigorous PBL by Design* is worthy of becoming a graduate-level text, while being, first and foremost, a readable and doable how-to guide for the interested teacher and leader.

Larry Ainsworth, Author and Consultant
Encinitas, CA

Michael McDowell's book provides powerful insights to ensure the conditions essential for PBL are present for increased impact on student learning. This magnificent book provides educators with practical ways to design authentic and everlasting learning.

Sarah Martin, Principal
Stonefields School, New Zealand

What a brilliant piece of literature that unravels and addresses the challenges of an educational concept that has familiarity to almost all educators! In his book, Dr. McDowell presents a doable means to making a positive change in learning by describing three design shifts—clarity, challenge, and culture. In this age of accountability when application of knowledge is required by academic standards, teachers of all grade levels can and will benefit from his approach to effectively implementing problem-based learning. The words *practical* and *inspirational* sum it up, as this guide will showcase PBL as a means to improving the instruction provided to learners, as well as making school a more meaningful place for both teachers *and* students.

Jan K. Hoegh, Associate Vice President
Marzano Research

This book is spot-on in being both practical and deeply informative for educators working to implement strong and lasting conditions that support PBL. Further, it provides a road map that can lead to significant improvement on student learning. It is a great example of just-in-time coaching!

John Deasy
Founding Partner, Cambiar
CEO, New Day New Year
Former Superintendent of LAUSD
Aspen Fellow
Executive Coach, Broad Foundation

Rigorous PBL by Design

Three Shifts for Developing Confident and Competent Learners

Michael McDowell

Foreword by John Hattie
Afterword by Suzie Boss

CORWIN
A SAGE Publishing Company

FOR INFORMATION:

Corwin
A SAGE Company
2455 Teller Road
Thousand Oaks, California 91320
(800) 233-9936
www.corwin.com

SAGE Publications Ltd.
1 Oliver's Yard
55 City Road
London EC1Y 1SP
United Kingdom

SAGE Publications India Pvt. Ltd.
B 1/I 1 Mohan Cooperative Industrial Area
Mathura Road, New Delhi 110 044
India

SAGE Publications Asia-Pacific Pte. Ltd.
3 Church Street
#10-04 Samsung Hub
Singapore 049483

Acquisitions Editor: Ariel Bartlett
Developmental Editor: Desirée A. Bartlett
Editorial Assistant: Kaitlyn Irwin
Production Editor: Melanie Birdsall
Copy Editor: Diane DiMura
Typesetter: Hurix Systems Pvt. Ltd.
Proofreader: Ellen Howard
Indexer: Molly Hall
Cover Designer: Gail Buschman
Marketing Manager: Anna Mesick

Printed in the United States of America

Library of Congress Cataloging-in-Publication Data

Names: McDowell, Michael, author.

Title: Rigorous PBL by design : three shifts for developing confident and competent learners / Michael McDowell ; foreword by John Hattie; afterword by Suzie Boss.

Other titles: Rigorous problem-based learning by design

Description: Thousand Oaks, California : Corwin, 2017. | Includes bibliographical references and index.

Identifiers: LCCN 2016044991 | ISBN 9781506359021 (pbk. : alk. paper)

Subjects: LCSH: Problem-based learning.

Classification: LCC LB1027.42 .M34 2017 | DDC 371.39— dc23 LC record available at https://lccn.loc.gov/2016044991

This book is printed on acid-free paper.

Certified Chain of Custody
Promoting Sustainable Forestry
www.sfiprogram.org
SFI-01268

SFI label applies to text stock

17 18 19 20 21 10 9 8 7 6 5 4 3 2 1

Contents

Download resources at
us.corwin.com/rigorouspblbydesign
under the "Preview" tab.

List of Online Resources

Resources and templates to facilitate PBL implementation can be found both in the book and online. Visit us.corwin.com/rigorouspblbydesign and click the "Preview" tab.

Foreword

Who could possibly not support problem-based learning! As outlined in this book, there are many positives: it is student centered, occurs in small groups, there is guidance and help from experts, authentic problems are involved, and there is much self-directed learning. There is a focus on problems, and not an overreliance on learning facts and rote learning and it can be fun. So many books already extol the virtues of problem-based learning (PBL), so why another? Moreover, there are hundreds of studies supporting PBL and showing it can enhance learning, so why another?

The reason is that the evidence is not so supportive of PBL. Analysis of 500 studies shows that the average impact of PBL on achievement is only 0.24—which rates PBL about 140th out of 200 influences on the Visible Learning list. It is possible for advocates to claim that PBL enhances learning, but the size of this effect is quite small and therefore contrary to the many overzealous claims for the essential place of PBL. (See the table on the next page.) Some of the effects are even negative, and there is remarkable variability.

Something seems not correct. How can a method that promises so much have such, on average, low impact? How can a method so often used in first-year medicine have such low impact (using the five meta-analyses in the table specific to medicine, the effect is only 0.08)? Is it fidelity of implementation, poor choice of problems, wrong students? A hint is provided when it is noted that the impact is much higher when introduced into fourth-year compared to first-year medicine.

In our recent synthesis of learning strategies, we (Hattie & Donoghue, 2016) demonstrated that the reason for this low effect seems to be related to introducing problem-based methods at the wrong time in the learning cycle. We based our work on a model that presupposes that there are three major parts to the learning cycle: surface or content learning, deep or relational learning, and transfer (near and far) of this learning. When PBL is introduced either to develop surface knowing, or before there is sufficient surface knowing, it has a close to zero and even a negative impact on learning. However, when problem-based learning is introduced after students have sufficient surface knowledge and are ready to enhance the deeper and relational notions, then the effects of PBL seem to increase. For example, Mark Albanese and Susan

PBL	YEAR	NUMBER OF STUDIES	NUMBER OF EFFECTS	EFFECT SIZE	FOCUS
1	Newman	2005	12	12	-0.30	PBL in medicine
2	Vernon & Blake	1993	8	28	-0.18	PBL at the college level
3	Schmidt, van der Molen, Te Winkel, & Wijnen	2009	10	90	-0.18	Constructivist problem-based learning on medical knowledge
4	Dochy, Segers, Van den Bossche, & Gijbels	2003	43	35	0.12	PBL on knowledge and skills
5	Walker & Shelton	2008	82	201	0.13	PBL across disciplines
6	Leary, Walker, Shelton, & Fitt	2013	94	213	0.24	PBL
7	Albanese & Mitchell	1993	11	66	0.27	PBL in medicine
8	Smith	2003	82	121	0.31	PBL in medicine
9	Gijbels, Dochy, Van den Bossche, & Segers	2005	40	49	0.32	PBL on assessment outcomes
10	Haas	2005	7	34	0.52	Teaching methods in algebra
11	Dagyar & Demirel	2015	98	98	0.76	PBL
12	Rosli, Capraro, & Capraro	2014	13	14	0.88	PBL
	Total/Average		500	961	**0.24**	

SOURCE: Hattie (2012).

Mitchell (1993) noted that increased years of exposure to medical education enhanced the effect of PBL. They argued that lack of experience (and lack of essential surface knowledge) leads the students to make more errors in their knowledge base, add irrelevant material to their explanations, and engage in backward reasoning (from the unknown to the givens), whereas experts engaged in forward reasoning (also see Gijbels, Dochy, Van den Bossche, & Segers, 2005; Gilhooly, 1990). Andrew Walker and Heather Leary (2009) also noted that novice PBL students tended to engage in far more backward-driven reasoning, which resulted in more errors during problem solving and may persist even after the educational intervention is complete. It is likely that problem-based learning works more successfully when students engage in forward reasoning, and this depends on having sufficient content knowledge to make connections.

We noted that deep understanding in problem-based learning requires a differentiated knowledge structure (Schwartz & Bransford, 1998), and this may need to be explicitly taught—as there is no assumption that students will see similarities and differences in contexts by themselves. There is a limit to what we can reasonably expect students to discover, and it may require teaching students to make predictions based on features that were told to them and that they may not notice on their own. Deliberate teaching of these surface features can offer a higher level of explanation that would be difficult or time-consuming to discover. A higher-level explanation is important because it provides a generative framework that can extend one's understanding beyond the specific cases that have been analyzed and experienced. On the other hand, the problems need not be too overly structured, as then students do not gain experience of searching out conceptual tools or homing in on particular cases of application (Perkins, 2014).

And this is a major reason to read this book, as Michael McDowell is very careful to make this critical claim—the right time, the right place, and the right instructions are key to the success of PBL. In Chapter 1, McDowell cites Jay McTighe and Grant Wiggins (2013) that students need to have a thorough understanding of core content knowledge by understanding facts and using skills within a discipline to ensure any method, including PBL will make a substantial difference. There also needs to be a sufficient level of confidence and trust by the students to explore uncertainties and to know what to do next when they do not know what to do. But McDowell is careful to not imply that PBL should be introduced only when students are "ready," as that then privileges those who already "can." He explores the structure of PBL tasks and groups to maximize the benefits for all students. In Chapter 2, he carefully crafts these developments by writing about "Scratching the Surface" and "Missing the Mark," and sets out a clear design structure for PBL.

The wrong message is that it is OK to provide students with unstructured or wicked problems and let them sort out solutions. No, the problems provided as part of PBL need to be carefully constructed; the intentions of going into "the pit" of learning need to be communicated to students near the beginning of the learning; and there needs to be clear alignment of the surface, deeper, and transfer parts of the learning cycle. There is indeed a "culture" that needs developing when implementing PBL. This culture, argues McDowell, is not a busy, buzzy hive of activity, not an overreliance on "authentic" tasks that engage students, not a snazzy techy solution—but a focus on making a change in learning via a relentless focus on clarity, challenge, and culture of learning the surface, the deeper, and the transfer aspects on the domain of knowledge to be learned. I applaud the way this book is structured as an investigation into the problem of problem-based learning, the focus on the optimal ways and times to introduce PBL, and the continual focus on the reasons to introduce PBL. PBL is not a good in itself, but it can be a desirable means to a learning end.

—John Hattie, Professor of Education
Director of the Melbourne Education Research Institute
University of Melbourne

Acknowledgments

There are so many people who have shaped the message in this book through their feedback to this text, their guidance and tutelage over the past twelve years, and their support of my leadership in bringing thoughts and ideas together to impact professional learning and ultimately the learning of children. From the first day I stepped into Napa New Tech High School, I had the privilege to work with and learn from some of the greatest minds and practitioners in the project-based arena including Mark Morrison, Paul Curtis, Megan Pacheco, Kevin Gant, Lee Fleming, Susan Schilling, Bob Pearlman, Tim Presiado, and the great people of Indiana. I am indebted to Suzie Boss, John Mergendoller, and John Larmer who have written powerful narratives that juxtaposed the literature with the practices needed for schools to implement impactful PBL.

I thank the teams, schools, and staff that I have had the pleasure of serving, learning from, and engaging with over the past decade. Thank you to my friends and colleagues in Indiana. Thank you to Joanna Mitchell, Steve Jennings, and the North Tahoe staff. Thank you to Laurie Kimbrel, the Ed Services team, and the incredible innovators who are still fighting for equity, a professional culture, and excellence for all children in the Tam District. I would like to thank the Ross school staff, community, and the Ross School Board of Trustees including John Longley, Todd Blake, Stephanie Robinson, Ann Sutro, Whit Gaither, and Josh Fisher for their unwavering support of my leadership and, more importantly, their commitment to public education and the learning and support of all children.

Some of the most important contributors in this work have been those who have provided a broader perspective outside the domain of PBL, a critical piece of research (or preponderance of research), a counternarrative, constructive criticism, or thoughtful commentary that allowed me to greatly ponder our work in PBL classrooms; they include Dylan Wiliam, Steven Brookfield, Robert Marzano, Sara Martin, Jay McTighe, and Jo Boaler. I would especially like to thank John Hattie who fundamentally influenced my thinking and my impact on educators and adults—I'm eternally grateful.

Corwin is a special place with absolutely wonderful people and I would like to thank Ariel Bartlett for her faith, honest feedback, and support in making this project happen. I would like to thank Desirée Bartlett for walking me over the finish line and having such a positive spirit. I also need to thank Kristin Anderson for her intoxicating optimism, support, and public accountability in getting the best out of everyone.

I would like thank my mother who modeled effective teaching and learning through her parenting and effective PBL with all of the children in Norman, Oklahoma, every night in our living room for over a decade.

Most of all I thank my wife, Quinn, and our two beautiful children (Asher, one year old, and Harper, six years old) for supporting me as I worked to craft the messages in this book, actually write the book, engage as a first year superintendent, and attempt to be a good father and husband. Thank you for your unwavering patience and for your calm affirmation that this book would make a lasting and positive impact on educators and children.

PUBLISHER'S ACKNOWLEDGMENTS

Corwin gratefully acknowledges the following reviewers for their editorial insight and guidance:

Polly Beebout, Science Teacher
CY Middle School
Casper, WY

Sandra K. Enger, University Faculty; Researcher; Consultant
University of Alabama in Huntsville
Huntsville, AL

Tom Hierck, Consultant/Author
Hierck Consulting
Gibsons, BC, Canada

Tara Howell, Vice Principal and Educational Leader
Junipero Serra High School
San Diego, CA

Dana B. Leonard, SPED High School Teacher
Ledford High School
Thomasville, NC

Tricia Peña, Adjunct Professor
Northern Arizona University
Vail, AZ

Ernie Rambo, Seventh-Grade US History Teacher
Walter Johnson Academy of International Studies
Las Vegas, NV

Leslie Standerfer, Principal
Estrella Foothills High School
Goodyear, AZ

Tim Tharrington, Sixth-Grade English Teacher
Wakefield Middle School
Raleigh, NC

Kara Vandas, Corwin Author and Consultant
Castle Rock, CO

About the Author

 **Michael McDowell, EdD,** serves as the superinten-
dent of the Ross School District in Ross, California.
Prior to serving as a superintendent, he served as
the associate superintendent of Instructional and
Personnel Services at the Tamalpais Union High
School District in Larkspur, California. Prior to his
role as a central office administrator, Dr. McDowell
was employed as the Principal of North Tahoe
High School, a Title I and California Distinguished
School. Dr. McDowell has been a leadership and
instructional coach for the New Tech Network,
consulting with schools, districts, higher-educational institutions, and state
departments on implementing effective problem- and project-based learning.
Dr. McDowell also designed and taught high school science and mathematics
at Napa New Tech High School and Ingrid B. Lacy Middle School in Pacifica,
California.

Dr. McDowell is a national presenter, speaking on instruction, learning,
leadership, and innovation. He is an author/consultant with Corwin, providing services in the Visible Learning Series and in Problem- and Project-Based
Learning. Dr. McDowell was a National Faculty member for the Buck
Institute of Education and an advisor to educational organizations focused
on equity, excellence, and innovation. His practical expertise in schools and
systems is complemented by his scholarly approach to leadership, learning,
and instruction. He holds a BS in environmental science and an MA in curriculum and instruction from the University of Redlands, and an EdD from
the University of La Verne, and he is a candidate for an MPA through the
Goldman School of Public Policy at the University of California, Berkeley.
His dissertation, titled *Group Leadership in the Project-Based Learning
Classroom*, focused on ensuring effective practices in PBL classrooms. He
has completed certification programs through Harvard University, the
California Association of School Business Officials, the American Association
of School Personnel Administrators, and Cognition Education. Michael and
his wife Quinn live in Northern California with their two children Harper
and Asher.

Introduction

In all affairs it's a healthy thing now and then to hang a question mark on things you have long taken for granted.

—Bertrand Russell

WHY I AM A PASSIONATE PROPONENT OF PBL

I am the father of two children (ages 1 and 6) and like most educators and parents, I want my children to be strong learners. I want them to possess a well-balanced and diverse level of knowledge and skills so that they can engage in, enjoy, and be successful in the 21st century. Furthermore, I want them to be advocates and partners with others for social justice. To meet these outcomes, I want my son and daughter to be immersed in learning environments that use engaging instructional methods such as problem- and project-based learning (PBL). I say this because I am convinced that when PBL is designed and delivered effectively, it has the potential to provide the deepest and most lasting impact on learning. Moreover, PBL has the potential to provide students with benefits, including, but not limited to,

- a sense of independence in their learning,

- a firsthand experience of how ideas can influence others,

- an understanding of the benefits of collaboration,

- a mindset for encountering and solving real-world problems,

- a belief that *everyone* can learn at high levels,

- an appreciation for the immense and complex diversity of people and ideas, and

- the ability to develop a depth of knowledge and skills that make up the gestalt of 21st century learning.

I want my children, all children, to have educational experiences that involve applying their skills to real problems that are important to them as learners and to the broader community. I want them to have "can't wait" moments of finding purpose in their work and autonomy in how they approach not only their learning but their life. I want them to infuse play, passion, and purpose in their education from K–12 through to college, career, and civil and familial engagements. The potential of PBL is beautiful because of the limitless ways to engage learners in their learning and the premise that all students can and should have influence over their learning and they can make an important contribution and impact on the world—now. However, in order for such outcomes to be brought forward, specific shifts in project design need to be present. The goal of this book is to present practical shifts in project design that teachers can apply in their classroom with confidence and enthusiasm to significantly impact student learning.

PBL DEFINED

PBL may be defined as a "series of complex tasks that include planning and design, problem solving, decision making, creating artifacts, and communicating results" (Mergendoller, Markham, Ravitz, & Larmer, 2006, p. 583). For the purposes of this text, project-based learning and problem-based learning are synonymous terms. This is supported in the literature as John Thomas (2000) argued, "the problem-based learning studies have all of the defining features of PBL" (p. 6), which include (Gijbels, Dochy, Van den Bossche, & Segers, 2005):

- Learning is student centered.

- Learning occurs in small groups.

- A tutor is present as facilitator or guide.

- Authentic problems are presented at the beginning of the learning sequence.

- The problems encountered are used as tools to achieve the required knowledge and the problem-solving skills necessary to eventually solve the problem.

- New information is acquired through self-directed learning.

This book is designed to enable teachers to apply the vast arsenal of synthesized research on learning to enhance project design and implementation so that they may substantially impact students' confidence in their learning and competence in the academic arena. It is important to note that PBL has not *yet* yielded the impact it is capable of. This unmet potential is perhaps due to the fact that PBL is often (though not always) driven by myths that orient the focus of teachers' and students' actions away from student learning of core academic content and that prevent the development of confidence in learning.

DISPELLING COMMON PBL MYTHS

Myth 1: "Sage on the stage" versus the "Guide on the side"

Truth: Teachers need to be adaptive

PBL myths are powerful; take for example the influential myth of the teacher's role in the classroom, which has been presented as a dichotomy between the "sage on the stage" versus the "guide on the side." The sage on the stage versus guide on the side dichotomy is not only false but also misleading to teachers. Facilitative (or guide on the side) approaches are highly valued in the PBL environment though they yield a relatively low effect on student learning. At the same time, the sage on the stage, which often refers to teachers lecturing to students while lacking modeling, guided practice, and checking for understanding, also equates to a low impact (Hattie, 2009). In reality, teachers need to be extremely adaptive in their teaching by constantly clarifying learning expectations, identifying where students are in their learning, and then, in light of student performance data, making instructional decisions that align with learner needs. As Andrew Larson (2016) argues,

> It is irresponsible to ask students to direct the course of their own learning if they don't have the appropriate framework for that content. Why would we [teachers] forego our own education, experience, and expertise when it comes to helping students unpack a concept, skill, or historical event? It is entirely possible and appropriate to ask students to apply higher thinking skills such as critical thinking, application, evaluation, and synthesis to content on their own, but we must provide them with the context and framework to do so. Otherwise we run the risk of having our students become curators of disconnected ideas, or worse, misconceptions.

Often more directive approaches are needed for students early on in the learning processes where teachers use direct instruction and give specific feedback on student tasks. Later in the learning, teachers are often found providing resources, offering feedback by way of self-reflective questions, and providing opportunities for students to make key decisions on demonstrating their understanding.

Myth 2: Students learn by doing.

Truth: Not without the proper support system

Other myths that permeate PBL classrooms include the idea that students "learn by doing." Such a statement has the potential to be dangerously reductive, as what children learn by doing is largely dependent on their prior knowledge and, as such, results in dramatically different outcomes for students (Nuthall, 2007).

Myth 3: PBL professional development should focus on the project.

Truth: PBL professional development should focus on learning.

PBL-related professional development often focuses teachers on forming student groups, teaching problem-solving strategies outside of academic content, focusing on the attributes of the project in terms of originality, and offering tools to enable students to be self-directed in acquiring new knowledge. Often, teachers are given tools on how to support students in managing projects, finding ways to present solutions to problems, and finding resources and talking with experts to understand and solve problems. As for quality control, teachers spend a significant amount of time focusing on project features such as the degree of authenticity or originality of the problem that will be presented to students, how groups will be developed, how students will present their information, and how they will access information. In sum, the focus of the professional development is largely on project management, project processes, and project group dynamics. The emphasis is on the *project* and enabling students to manage a project process. In contrast, I argue that we need to deemphasize the term *project* in project-based learning and embolden the term *learning*. Quality projects are those that support teachers in ensuring that students are learning one year's worth of academic content in one year's time and are building their capacity to understand and take action over their learning. This does not require that students are in groups to learn (though they should collaborate) or teachers are tutors (though they may be, once students have developed a level of mastery in their learning), or that self-direction is qualified by acquiring new information in isolation (in fact, teachers should use more directive methods to enable students to learn content when learning something new). Project management has a time and place in projects but it is secondary to the learning of core content and confidence.

Myth 4: Learning depends on whether you position PBL as the main course or the dessert.

Truth: Learning depends on how you design PBL, regardless of whether it is the main course or the dessert.

See "The Three Design Shifts: Clarity, Challenge, and Culture" on page 6 for more on this.

PBL WITH A FOCUS ON LEARNING AND CONFIDENCE IN LEARNING

This book aims to help educators focus specifically on those actions that have a high probability of substantially impacting student learning in the areas of content literacy and confidence in their learning. Specifically, this book walks educators through practical steps that ensure students have a balance of surface, deep, and transfer understanding of content knowledge and skill and that they have a command over their own learning. In order to do this, teachers need to provide specific actions, either through direct teaching or other means, to ensure that students are able to master important learning outcomes and achieve advanced understanding through high-level, rigorous work. For example, more time needs to be spent on identifying a student's current understanding in relation to academic expectations and providing targeted instruction. Even more, teachers need to design projects that emphasize reading, writing, and talking rather than cutting, pasting, and designing software-based content in the PBL environment. After reading this book, educators will have the tools necessary to assess student performance, target instruction, and help students make the necessary connections between basic-level understandings and the larger questions raised by their projects.

Our work has to be focused completely on a child's learning. And that is the focus of this book—to illustrate how to design projects that focus on substantially enhancing student content knowledge and skill and simultaneously building students' self-confidence in their learning. As such, this book enables teachers and learners to gather defensible and dependable evidence to determine their efficacy on learning. Overall, this book highlights three major shifts (i.e., clarity, challenge, and culture) in project design that have a high probability of enhancing student confidence (assessment-capable learning, growth mindset, and collaboration) and competence (surface, deep, and transfer). When designed effectively, PBL has a high probability of substantially impacting *all learners.*

PBL FOR ALL

In the chapters that follow, limitations of and suggested fixes to the PBL method will be discussed. In particular, PBL has been shown, time and time again, to yield minimal gains in student achievement at the early stages of learning (Hattie, 2009). When learners need basic knowledge and skills, inquiry- and facilitation-based approaches are weak in leveraging learning. In fact, problem- and project-based learning is one of the least impactful methods in existence at this level. When learners are ready for more advanced knowledge and skills, such methods are ideal. The conundrum that a teacher faces is that all learners need both basic and advanced learning to be fully prepared to engage in rich critical-thinking tasks and situations required for the 21st century.

Simultaneously, there is an inherent danger in providing PBL only to those who are "ready" for it. Too often the narrative of ready is linked to biases, and often deficit viewpoints lead to a particular diagnosis that is largely self-fulfilling. Martin Haberman (1991) wrote an article titled "The Pedagogy of Poverty Versus Good Teaching," which argued that certain instructional methods are offered only to those of privilege. When certain groups of people are offered a deeper-learning method, regardless of the method's inherent blemishes, a continued narrative of intelligence and selection is ensured. Inherent or explicit expectations are interwoven in all classes, and a lack of democratization of access to methods is widely apparent to children. The learning lives of students are often filtered by how adults separate them, what privileges are provided through rules and methods, and expectations that are implicitly and explicitly shown from daily behavior.

There are many students regardless of race, economic status, and gender who could be harmed by methods that are not effective at yielding strong results at the early stages of learning. Many students are particularly vulnerable to the inherent instructional challenges of deeper-learning models; and at the same time these students are vulnerable to the absence of the expectations, challenges, and opportunities that are inclusive of such methods. Children and adults require substantial background knowledge and skills to think critically and solve authentic problems in varying contexts. Children and adults require high expectations, support, and access to quality content. The argument here is to retool such methods to ensure surface and deep learning are maximized in deeper-learning methods and that all students have the opportunity to experience the inherent joys and academic impact of PBL. In fact, even though Hattie's own published research shows a low effect size for PBL, Hattie himself has enthusiastically endorsed this book substantiating the assertion that PBL can be designed and implemented in strategic ways that will dramatically increase the potential for student learning and improvement in student academic achievement.

THE THREE DESIGN SHIFTS: CLARITY, CHALLENGE, AND CULTURE

A long-standing axiom of PBL is that its success in enabling students to learn advanced content and skills depends on how it is positioned—is it the main course, or is it the dessert (Larmer & Mergendoller, 2010a)? The main course approach involves beginning a unit using PBL and teaching content and skills within the project. In contrast, the dessert approach involves the teacher focusing sharply on the content and skill-building first, and then applying those skills to the project. The focus on the placement of the project is a typical myth in the PBL community that is misguided and shifts our focus away from learning. Whether you chose to implement PBL as the main course or the dessert doesn't matter when it comes down to student learning. (This book uses the main course approach, as it is the most popular and recommended approach in the PBL community.) What matters is (1) the clarity of learning outcomes and success criteria, (2) challenging students at their learning level (providing targeted instruction in light of student assessment data), and (3) ensuring a culture that focuses on students taking ownership over their learning and acting as a resource to others in their learning. To simplify, the ingredients of a successful project are clarity, challenge, and culture. Chapters 3, 4, and 5 of this book each focus on one of these essential ingredients.

In order to focus on the learning in PBL, it is imperative that educators design projects from the beginning with the three aforementioned design shifts in mind. The term *shift* is used here to emphasize the point that teachers must reorient their focus and practices away from the projects themselves toward the learning of students.

Briefly, these are the three design shifts:

- **Design Shift I—Clarity:** Students need to be absolutely clear on what they are expected to learn, where they are in their learning, and what next steps they need to take to advance their learning. Their understanding and use of content knowledge and skills should transcend any project situation or context.

- **Design Shift II—Challenge:** Students need to have a consistent balance of surface, deep, and transfer knowledge and to thoroughly understand and apply content to real-world challenging problems. Each level of content complexity requires different instructional interventions, tasks, and feedback.

- **Design Shift III—Culture:** Students need to be able to talk about their learning, monitor their learning, advocate for next steps in their learning, and be a part of a culture that focuses on and models such efforts.

SPECIAL FEATURES

With this book, you will find a specific focus on designing projects that embed the three shifts to build student competence and confidence. You will read through the perspectives of practitioners in the field as well as researchers and advocates who discuss the critical importance of the shifts illuminated in this text. The tools and methods here will help you as the project designer to move from good to great by focusing on clarity, challenge, and culture. In this book, you will find the following special features:

- A unique focus on learning competence and confidence in learning.

- The three design shifts—clarity, challenge, and culture—provide a framework for successful PBL implementation for classrooms, schools, and districts.

- Each section of the book is thoroughly research based, providing multiple sources to substantiate the benefits and successful strategies of PBL.

- The *four questions* provide an expedient, easy-to-remember guide that students can use to take ownership of their own learning at each stage of their learning.

- The easy-to-follow steps guide you in applying formative assessment and formative teaching practices to ensure that your students succeed at all levels of learning (surface, deep, and transfer).

- The *Questions for Reflection* at the end of each chapter will help you think about how these strategies apply to your own particular school and district setting.

- Each chapter ends with *Next Steps* that encourage you to apply the content of each chapter to get you started in improving your own PBL practices.

- There are multiple examples of sample projects and problems for teachers to use as templates for their own curriculum development.

- Educators who are interested in implementation can find valuable insights from the *Voices From the Trenches* sections where educators reflect on their own particular experience with schoolwide PBL implementation.

- *Activities* will help you create your own learning intentions, driving questions, entry events, and all other aspects of thorough PBL planning.

- Examples, tables, checklists, sample calendars, student activities, protocols, rubrics, and images to facilitate understanding and application of the material are included.

- *Online resources*, such as templates, checklists, and other resources are available both in the book and online for you to use in your own practice.

- *Appendices* offer four very detailed project plans that span grade levels and content areas showing how all of the pieces of the book fit together when designing a project.

- The *Glossary* provides definitions to key words that will aid in understanding all of the nuanced aspects of PBL implementation.

CHAPTER 1

Focusing on Confidence and Competence in Learning

If we are to understand how teaching relates to learning, we have to begin at the closest point to that learning, and that is students' experience.

—Graham Nuthall (2001)

CONFIDENT AND COMPETENT STUDENTS AT WORK: SIR FRANCIS DRAKE HIGH SCHOOL

Nestled between a range of rolling mountains in Marin County, sits a high school with a teacher who routinely engages in conversations with learners about their learning. When you enter Mrs. Mall's classroom at Sir Francis Drake High School, students (or *learners* as they are called) track their own academic performance, discuss their performance levels with her and their peers, seek feedback from others, and codevelop next steps to improve. On any given day, an observer in the classroom can sense that learners value feedback, are emotionally prepared for criticism, and are clearly able to balance perseverance of engaging in the same strategy to accomplish tasks while also considering new strategies that may result in a better solution. When prompted, learners can explain their progress by discussing the level of complexity of their learning. For example, students can describe whether they are learning surface-level (basic) knowledge, connecting knowledge to other ideas, or transferring their understanding to new problems. In addition to being able to articulate the level and depth of their learning, they are also able to relate their current learning to overall goals and discuss the steps they need to improve. In other words, they have a clear sense of where they are, where they are going, and what to do next. This describes what John Hattie (2009) has termed "Visible Learning."

Mrs. Mall plays an integral role in the process of the students' learning journey. She does so by regularly tracking performance, providing feedback, prompting critical assessment of strategies, and asking the students to reflect not only on their own performance but also on how they are supporting each other's learning. Mrs. Mall and the students have developed a shared understanding of content expectations, strategies used to improve learning, common agreements on dispositions that enable effective learning (such as how to handle failure), and effective means to dialogue (such as giving and receiving feedback).

At the conclusion of the semester, the students in the class were asked to identify their reflections from the class, resulting in the following comments:

> "I'm honest with where I am in this class. This way of assessment has completely made me feel alright with being 'in the pit' because I know that I am not stuck there and that I can get myself out of it. I really appreciate all that you have done to make us feel comfortable with progress."

> "'Be open to struggling' . . . Before this class I was not open to struggling at all, so this took me a while to get used to."

> "Now I know that I can get myself out of the pit, so I feel comfortable being in it! I just wish it was this way in the rest of my classes."

> "My annotations and thoughts on written pieces were at about a 1 level at the beginning of the semester, but with guidance in class and a lot of practice I have grown to getting a 4 on the last annotation [out of 4.0]. Next semester I hope to grow further."

CONFIDENCE IN LEARNING ATTRIBUTES

Such experiences and student feedback directly relate to confidence in learning and echo the sentiment of Seymour Papert when he said, "The kind of knowledge children most need is the knowledge that will help them get more knowledge" (cited in Way & Beardon, 2003, p. 68). The statements of the students in Mrs. Mall's classroom shine a light on core attributes of confidence in learning, including having a growth mindset, becoming assessment-capable learners, and collaborating with peers (see Figure 1.1).

Growth Mindset

Learning does not occur without great effort, perseverance, and patience. This process begins with a belief, or "mindset" that intelligence is malleable and can be changed through very specific actions. Having a growth mindset is in direct contrast with the belief that intelligence is fixed and immutable regardless of effort, persistence, and change in improvement strategy. The growth mindset enables all learners to understand that learning at high levels

FIGURE 1.1 Confidence in Learning

Confidence in Learning

Learners . . .	Learners . . .	Learners . . .
understand what makes a strong learner and believe they and others can improve.	understand how they learn and how to increase learning, and use that information to improve.	use the power of peer-to-peer interactions to enhance their learning and that of others.
Growth Mindset	**Assessment-Capable Learners**	**Learning With Others**

---

is achievable for all children and that by using feedback to identify next steps, reflecting on performance to improve, and accepting guidance they can improve their own learning. Additionally, a growth mindset enables learners to see mistakes as part of the process of learning and, as such, learners are often more willingly to seek and accept feedback.

A growth mindset couples a set of beliefs that drive the right actions necessary to meet challenging outcomes. A growth mindset may be more appropriately named a growth *mind to action* set whereby students take action to improve. As Eduardo Briceño (2015) argues, "[S]tudents often haven't learned that working hard involves thinking hard, which involves reflecting on and changing our strategies so we become more and more effective learners over time, and we need to guide them to come to understand this." Strategies such as organizing and transforming ideas, seeking help, goal setting, and developing self-consequences are all metacognitive and study skill strategies that can have a substantial impact on learning (Lavery, 2008) and should be coupled with the belief that such strategies can improve a child's learning. This *belief to action* system is critical to drive students to improve their learning through practice and to develop and reinforce the idea that through effort and strategy, they can improve their learning. Often students develop this belief system through their actions. As Doug Reeves (2009) states, "Behavior precedes belief" (p. 44) and as such, teachers should consider using strategies that enable students to specifically measure, discuss, and improve their own learning.

Many schools have translated the growth mindset belief system to specific dispositions, habits, and strategies to improve learning. For example, at Stonefield School in New Zealand, students (or *learners* as they are called at Stonefield) have identified strategies such as using questioning, being determined, being self-aware, reflecting on learning, and connecting ideas as important for learners to improve their own learning. In essence, the growth mindset is much more encompassing than expecting students to use raw persistence, grit, and work ethic to improve. The important point is that students must believe not only that they themselves can learn at high levels but that they can and will do so through deliberate actions. One key way to instill this growth mindset is by developing students' assessment capabilities whereby they monitor their progress and take action to improve.

Assessment-Capable Learners

Assessment-capable learners have a specific set of behaviors and skills that are associated with monitoring, evaluating, and improving (e.g., through feedback) learning. This set of behaviors allows learners to understand both expectations of learning and their performance, and to identify and act on data that drives next steps in the learning process. Learners have knowledge of what drives effective learning, a language to describe their level of learning, and a number of strategies they use to improve their learning. They are able to work with teachers and others to ensure alignment of current performance and craft subsequent actions.

Assessment-capable learners "think hard" by reflecting on the strategies they are using to advance their learning, seeking feedback from others, and monitoring performance to continually improve. In particular, assessment-capable learners monitor their performance by ensuring they can answer the following questions:

- Where am I going in my learning?

- Where am I now in my learning?

- What's the next thing I need to improve in my learning?

- How do I improve my learning and that of others?

Having assessment capabilities has a significant impact on improving learning (Hattie, 2009). Many schools around the world have incorporated assessment-capable strategies to enable children to develop responsibilities for their own learning. For example, in the Mangere Bridge School, students take part in data teams to review their performance levels. Through these discussions, students receive feedback from teachers and peers on their performance; reflect on their own performance; advocate for resources, instructional support, and time to enhance their learning; and create a series of actions for improvement.

The means by which to measure one's performance is clearly a motivator outside of the academic arena. In Patrick Lencioni's (2014) book *Three Signs of a Miserable Job*, he illustrates that a key sign of job dissatisfaction included "immeasurability." Lencioni described this sign as the frustration employees have when they are unable to track their progress and lack a clear understanding of their performance relative to work expectations. Daniel Pink (2011), in his popular text *Drive*, cites mastery—or the pursuit of developing one's skills and knowledge over time to reach beyond proficiency—as one the key factors influencing human motivation. Clearly, humans like to keep track of their performance and work to improve. Engaging in pedagogy that ensures students develop the capabilities to assess their own learning will provide them with the skills necessary to continually engage in their learning and will be invaluable in their future careers.

Collaboration

Collaborative learners recognize the tremendous power of the social aspect of learning and the need and desire to enhance each other's learning through shared understanding, debate, and collective action. Learning is very much a social experience, and a student's confidence is inextricably linked to the power of working with, supporting, and learning from peers and teachers. In this text, the *collaboration* is defined as the means by which students act as learning resources for one another to improve individual and collective learning.

If particular practices are not established that focus on enhancing individual and collective learning, it is extremely difficult for learners to actualize a growth mindset or action set and develop the skills to be an assessment-capable learner. The challenge is that feedback from peers is often incorrect (Nuthall, 2007) and often absent in classrooms (McDowell, 2009). The means to facilitate the level of engagement required is also difficult for teachers, as it demands a unique set of skills that are rarely taught in school- or district-level professional development (McDowell, 2009). The establishment and use of common and explicit agreements and structured protocols that are focused on measuring performance, sharing and discussing ideas, and giving and receiving feedback can rapidly improve collaboration among and between students. Moreover, collaboration among students can be enhanced when teachers and staff model similar group behaviors in school.

Collectively, the attributes of confidence (i.e., a growth mindset, assessment-capable learning, and collaboration) yield substantial gains on student academic performance. In fact, assessment-capable learning has one of the greatest effects on student learning ever researched (Hattie, 2009). Carol Dweck (2007) found that students who have a growth mindset outperform others who believe their intelligence is fixed. Leveraging peers to give and receive feedback has been found to very beneficial to students in their academic work and relationship development (Nuthall, 2007). Collectively these three attributes enable students to think and feel confident in their learning and, accordingly, improve academically.

COMPETENCE IN LEARNING LEVELS:
SURFACE, DEEP, AND TRANSFER

Confidence in learning is intertwined with the development of a student's knowledge and skill set. Mrs. Mall expected her students to build a core set of knowledge and skills, connect that learning to other ideas, and apply that information to various situations. She stressed the importance of having the breadth and depth of knowledge and skill required to address real-world problems. By design, she ensured that students developed both competency and confidence.

The competencies needed in today's knowledge-based economy require students to develop the ability to use knowledge in ambiguous, social, and dynamic situations. Today's workforce puts a premium on employees who have the ability to solve problems, understand and use data, and engage in team-based situations (Bersin, 2014). Likewise, today's employees demand similar expectations and experiences from their employers (Wagner, 2012; Wiliam, 2011; Zhao, 2012). As such, employees and employers are attracted to people and environments where meaningful tasks, collaboration, and problem solving are present.

It is imperative that schools develop students' abilities to transfer their learning and skills to each new experience and task. Hanna Dumont, David Istance, and Francisco Benavides (2010) state,

> Many scholars agree that the ultimate goal of learning and associated teaching in different subjects is to acquire *adaptive expertise*—i.e. the ability to apply meaningfully-learned knowledge and skills flexibly and creatively in different situations. This goes beyond mastery or routine expertise in a discipline. Rather it involves the willingness and ability to change core competencies and continually expand the breadth and depth of one's expertise. (p. 3; emphasis in original)

In order to be competent in learning, students need to be capable and knowledgeable on three levels: *surface level*, *deep level*, and *transfer level*. To develop the application of knowledge and skills to new situations, students must possess a thorough knowledge base within and across academic domains (McTighe & Wiggins, 2013). In other words, students need to have a thorough understanding of core content knowledge by understanding facts and using skills within a discipline (surface-level knowledge). They must also be able to relate facts and skills within a discipline (deep-level knowledge). And finally, they need to have the ability to extend those ideas to other disciplines and situations (transfer-level knowledge; see Figure 1.2).

Surface-Level Knowledge

Surface-level knowledge refers to learners' ability to understand single or multiple ideas, but they are limited by the relationship of ideas and to a larger principle or skill set. They are building knowledge and building skills.

FIGURE 1.2 Levels of Learning

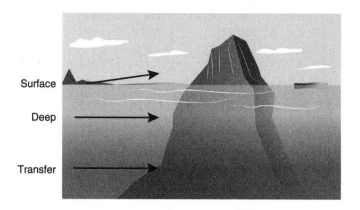

IMAGE SOURCE: Pixabay/Matty Simpson

Deep-Level Knowledge

Deep-level knowledge refers to a learner's ability to relate multiple ideas. It also describes the ability to understand similarities and differences between concepts and skills. At the deep level of knowledge, students understand how specific ideas are related to the underlying principles of a discipline. They are relating ideas and relating skills.

Transfer-Level Knowledge

Transfer-level knowledge refers to a learner's ability to apply basic and complex understanding and skills to challenging problems within and between contexts. With transfer-level knowledge, learners are able to link ideas in new ways and can predict, evaluate, and generalize across contexts. They are applying knowledge and applying skills.

The critical challenge is for teachers to find instructional approaches that balance surface and deep learning and also provide opportunities for students to transfer their understanding to real-world problems. As John Hattie (2009) states,

> There needs to be a major shift from an overreliance on surface information and a reduced emphasis that the goal of education is deep understanding or development of thinking skills, towards a balance of surface and deep learning, leading to students more successfully constructing defensible theories of knowing . . . . [T]he choice of classroom instruction and learning activities to maximize these outcomes are hallmarks of quality teaching. (p. 28)

Dylan Wiliam (2011) writes, "As teachers, we are not interested in our students' ability to do what we have taught them to do. We are only interested in their ability to apply their newly acquired knowledge to a similar but different context" (p. 60). Research has found substantial gains in student learning when teachers design curriculum, assess learning, and guide student learning across surface- and deep-level outcomes (see Figure 1.3; Hattie, 2009).

FIGURE 1.3 Conclusion of Research on Interventions Related to Student Improvement

Taking a Closer Look Into the Research

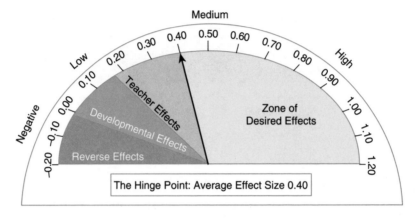

Professor Hattie's synthesis of the meta-analysis research found that almost everything we do in and around classrooms works (95%) to improve classroom instruction. The average effect of all variables on learning is at a 0.40 (or the hinge point). The figure shows the range of effects from the 800-plus meta-analyses studied.

IMAGE SOURCE: Hattie (2009).

PBL AS A VEHICLE TO BUILD CONFIDENCE AND COMPETENCE IN LEARNING

Educators continually search for practical ways to effectively and efficiently improve learning for children. Although Hattie's research indicates that almost every intervention works (2009), the key is for educators to focus on the interventions that promise the most substantial growth in academic performance. One option available to educators is to implement the methods of PBL into their classroom. Problem- and project-based learning are methods that aim for developing deeper-learning outcomes including transfer-level expectations (competence) as well as affective outcomes that encompass the attributes of confidence (McDowell, 2009). Moreover, PBL is an approach to teaching that has the potential to codify the practices that have the most impact on learning and is a succinct and doable approach for practitioners.

> PBL is an approach to teaching that has the potential to codify the practices that have the most impact on learning and is a succinct and doable approach for practitioners.

Research has shown that students within schools that use PBL as their primary methodology, on average, outperform their peers in traditional classrooms on state and national tests (Zeiser, Taylor, Rickles, Garet, & Segeritz, 2014). However, according to Hattie's (2009) findings, PBL in and of itself has yet to yield the substantial achievement gains that schools are aiming for. For instance, problem-based learning and other inquiry methods have shown a minimal effect at improving surface-level acquisition (effect size = 0.15 and 0.30 respectively). Although the research has not shown PBL to have a significantly positive effect on surface-level knowledge, it does show that PBL has a substantial impact at deeper levels of learning (effect size = 0.68). In order to achieve both goals—surface-level mastery as well as deeper-level knowledge—educators at the leader level and classroom level need to design and implement PBL by incorporating practices that have shown a consistently high effect on learning. This happens sometimes; with an intentional focus on design, this desired effect could be more common.

> In order to achieve both goals—surface-level mastery as well as deeper-level knowledge—educators at the leader level and classroom level need to design and implement PBL by incorporating practices that have shown a consistently high effect on learning.

CONCLUSION

To ensure student success, educators need to apply specific practices that have a high probability for enhancing confidence and competency in learning. *When designed and implemented effectively using the three design shifts*, problem- and project-based learning have the potential to support students both in efficiently acquiring surface-level knowledge, deeper-level learning, and desired affective outcomes (such as growth mindset, assessment capabilities, and collaboration skills), and in emulating practices sought for in the careers of tomorrow.

QUESTIONS FOR REFLECTION

- What evidence do you have from student behavior (language, actions) that they are modeling a growth mindset? How are you expressing these behaviors in your own actions as a teacher? How do you demonstrate the importance of a growth mindset in the classroom? How do your management, assessment (including grading), and instructional approaches illustrate to students that errors are welcomed in your classroom?

- How have you ensured that students are

  developing assessment capabilities?

  using peers to support one another in understanding their learning?

  giving and receiving feedback to move their learning forward?

  monitoring their progress to understand what is and isn't working for their own learning?

- How do you support students in discussing surface, deep, and transfer learning?

- What do you think are the strengths and weaknesses of PBL in developing competence and confidence?

NEXT STEPS

- Determine the level of clarity in learning expectations within your current projects or lessons by asking students the following three questions:

  Where are you going?

  Where are you now?

  What next steps are you going to take?

  Through this process, determine if the answers are about compliance, completion, and context or about learning goals, current performance levels based on assessment, and next steps as related to enhancing performance.

- Review your current unit of study or project and identify the levels of challenge for students.

  Are you able to identify surface-, deep-, and transfer-level learning?

  Do you have evidence (i.e., assessments, lessons, rubrics) that these levels exist and are important?

  Do the students know this as well? How do you know?

- Ask students the following:

  What intentional actions have we put into place that help you understand

  > *your learning?*

  > *that errors are welcomed?*

  > *that peer feedback is valued?*

  > *that we value learning as demonstrated through language and our behaviors?*

CHAPTER 2

Designing PBL for Student Confidence and Competence

All models are wrong, some are useful.

—George Edward Pelham Box

One of the most widely used and popular ways of qualifying problem- and project-based learning is through the use of the *Gold Standard PBL: Essential Project Design Elements,* published by the Buck Institute of Education. In that book, John Larmer, John Mergendoller, and Suzie Boss (2015) identify seven Essential Project Design Elements including: (1) a challenging problem or question, (2) sustained inquiry, (3) authenticity, (4) student voice and choice, (5) reflection, (6) critique and revision, and (7) a public product. Figure 2.1 briefly illustrates the defining qualities of these elements.

As stated earlier, PBL may be defined as a "series of complex tasks that include planning and design, problem solving, decision making, creating artifacts, and communicating results" (Mergendoller, Markham, Ravitz, & Larmer, 2006, p. 583). Collectively, the quality criteria in Figure 2.1 ensure teachers align complex tasks, planning and design, problem solving, decision making, creating artifacts, and communicating results with a challenging problem or driving question. Ideally, the driving question requires students to understand the central concepts and principles of a discipline. Typically, the driving question is presented at the beginning of the learning sequence and is used to foster a student's ability to connect prior knowledge and project activities to the academic outcomes of the project. Teachers often implement a diverse set of teaching methods to support students in addressing the driving question and presenting their solutions. Projects that are designed with fidelity to the Gold Standard Elements often include sustained inquiry, the use of critique and revision, and opportunities for reflection. Moreover, solutions are typically related to real-world problems, require multiple perspectives to

FIGURE 2.1 Summary of Quality PBL Criteria

Gold Standard PBL requires:

- **Challenging Problem or Question:** Students are presented with "an engaging problem or question that makes learning more meaningful for students. They are not gaining knowledge to remember it; they are learning because they have a real need to know something, so they can use this knowledge to solve a problem or answer a question that matters to them."

- **Sustained Inquiry:** "In PBL, inquiry is iterative; when confronted with a challenging problem or questions, students ask questions, find resources to help answer them, then ask deeper questions—and the process repeats until a satisfactory solution or answer is developed."

- **Authenticity:** Relates to the "real-world" aspects of the project including the context of the problem; engaging in real tasks, processes, and tools; ensuring the project will have an impact on others; and relating to learners' own interests.

- **Student Voice and Choice:** "Students have input . . . over many aspects of a project . . . including how they want to investigate it, demonstrate what they have learned, and how they will share their work."

- **Reflection:** "Reflections on the content knowledge and understanding gained help students solidify what they have learned and think about how it might apply elsewhere, beyond the project."

- **Critique and Revision:** "Students should be taught how to give and receive constructive peer feedback that will improve project processes and products."

- **Public Products:** Are used to ensure preparedness of the student, are vehicles to discuss the learning that has taken place, and are tangible evidence of the solution to a problem or answer to a driving question.

SOURCE: Adapted from Larmer, Mergendoller, & Boss (2015).

solve, combine the use of knowledge and skills across disciplines, and are anchored in a public presentation (Brooks & Brooks, 1993; Driscoll, 1994; Duffy & Jonassen, 1991). Such elements are revered as high-quality standards of PBL.

MAKE PBL EFFECTIVE

One of the greatest challenges for a classroom teacher is in interpreting each criterion and then deciding how to design a project that makes a substantial impact on learning. A project that meets all of the Gold Standard criteria might still fall short of promoting student learning at surface, deep, and transfer levels. For example, to fulfill the critique and revision criterion, teachers may interpret this to mean that they should focus on providing feedback to students. But the type of feedback provided (e.g. task, process, or self-regulation) has a varied effect depending on the level of learning required (surface, deep, or transfer). That is, feedback is found to have a substantial effect on student learning only when the type of feedback is directly aligned with a student's level of understanding (Hattie & Timperley, 2007). As John Hattie and Helen Timperley state, "Feedback has no effect in a vacuum," (p. 82) and as such, must be directly aligned with the learning needs (surface, deep, or transfer) of a student. For instance, students who are at the transfer level of learning would be better served with feedback geared toward self-monitoring their performance than task-based feedback (more on this in Chapter 4).

Specific targeted practices must be thoughtfully designed, implemented, and inspected to meet competence and confidence expectations. As such, there are a few pitfalls to be aware of when designing and implementing projects for surface- to deep- to transfer-level learning and building a student's confidence. We will review two major types of pitfalls in PBL design including "Scratching the Surface" and "Missing the Mark." Scratching the Surface pitfalls are typical errors that teachers make when they meet Gold Standard Elements but lack sufficient implementation of the three design shifts stated in this book (clarity, challenge, and culture; see Figure 2.1). Missing the Mark pitfalls are those errors where the three design shifts are completely absent from project design and project implementation and typically lack Gold Standard Elements.

FIGURE 2.2 Project Snapshot: Nairobi National Park Project

Nairobi National Park is one of the best examples of the conflicts surrounding wildlife and humans. The park is almost completely fenced in except for the southern boundary. Many people in Kenya want the southern boundary to be fenced in order to reduce public safety threats and allow for housing and transit. However, fencing the park would create one of the largest zoos in the world, creating significant challenges to the normal behavior of wild animals. Drawing on what we know about carrying capacity, food chains, and food webs, the proposal for fencing in the park might negatively affect the animals that live there. On the other hand, given the exponential growth of the Kenyan capital, the demand for housing land around the park will continue to rise.

▶ **Key Question**

How should the Kenyan Government approach such an important issue?

IMAGE SOURCE: Wikimedia Commons/Mkimemia

Scratching the Surface

The Nairobi National Park Project (see Figure 2.2) was designed for students to understand how specific principles of biology and environmental science interplay in a real life situation and how to apply those principles into a feasible solution. Depending on how the project is designed and implemented, the Nairobi project may or may not have a substantial impact on student learning. It has the potential to meet the Gold Standard criteria: The project includes a driving question that requires knowledge to solve the problem, a standard set of questions to engage in inquiry, and a real problem. It infers voice and choice in designing a solution as a specific product for students to complete is not specified, and there is room for reflection to be carried out to meet project tasks. The challenge here is not that the Gold Standard Elements have been met but rather the degree to which students learn content at surface, deep, and transfer levels and enhance their confidence in learning.

If designed ineffectively, students may struggle with understanding the core learning intentions and success criteria of the project and may spend more time focused on the context of the project (i.e., Nairobi National Park) rather than the biology and environmental science standards. Moreover, if teachers have not planned for continuous assessment of learning and prepared for targeting specific instructional and feedback strategies for learners based on performance, then one can expect a lack of substantive growth in learning. Students could end up spending their time Googling the park, Googling carrying capacity, Googling food chains, talking about their Googling with others in groups, and creating a PowerPoint or trifold in just a few hours. Teachers may spend a significant amount of time managing project tasks, finding resources, and constructing processes for students to engage in inquiry. If limited to project management, inquiry, and self- or group-directed efforts alone, the project could meet the essentials of project-based learning and, at the same time, require minimal cognitive demand and lack the necessary teacher actions to yield a high impact on learning. To move from scratching the surface to a deeper level of design, we must ask the following:

> Learning intentions are best thought of as brief statements that explicitly describe what students should know (i.e., content) and be able to do (i.e., skill).
>
> Success criteria specify what students must demonstrate at the surface, deep, and transfer levels to meet learning intentions.

- Have teachers designed and clarified to learners clear learning intentions and success criteria that are aligned with content complexity (i.e., surface, deep, and transfer) and independent of context?

- Are teachers prepared to continually identify where students are in their understanding relative to learning intentions and success criteria?

- In light of the evidence they find, have teachers prepared for actions (e.g., instructional approaches and types of feedback) that target student learning needs?

- Are we building students' capacity to identify their level of understanding and take action to improve their learning and that of others?

The intention here is to articulate that the quality criteria we are looking for in a methodology must be specifically targeted to students' learning. For example, John Larmer, John Mergendoller, and Suzie Boss (2015) argue, "In project based learning, it is the project itself, carefully planned by the teacher that structures student inquiry and guides learning activities towards project goals" (p. 39). This book is supportive of the project structure to initially promote inquiry and guide learning activities. Ideally, the project would be anchored in key learning intentions and success criteria and have established tasks that scaffold learning. However, this book contends that it is not the project itself that structures and guides learning activities toward project goals. Rather, student performance data and prior knowledge relative to learning goals throughout the project are what structure and guide learning activities toward project goals. Moreover, such information forms instructional decisions throughout the project to move learning forward. Stated differently, designing a project to structure inquiry *is a good starting place* for engaging learners. That being said, what is essential is continual assessment of learner progress and the subsequent adaptation of instruction and feedback throughout the project based on learner performance.

To go deeper, teachers must clarify the learning intentions and success criteria, use inquiry to identify student progress, target instruction and feedback according to a learner's performance level, and develop a culture that focuses on understanding and using performance data to improve.

To go deeper, teachers must clarify the learning intentions and success criteria, use inquiry to identify student progress, target instruction and feedback according to a learner's performance level, and develop a culture that focuses on understanding and using performance data to improve. When these shifts are instituted, structured inquiry is understood as a guide for teachers and students to understand performance relative to learning goals, to identify the most effective teaching and learning strategies, and to find tasks that best showcase learning. In this way, the focus is specifically on the learning, not the project. Instead of just scratching the surface, aim to design and implement projects that require students and teachers to understand performance relative to learning goals, target instruction in light of performance, and develop a culture conducive to discussing learning.

Missing the Mark

In addition to scratching the surface pitfalls, teachers must be wary of project design and implementation that lacks the ingredients necessary to enhance learning of core content knowledge and build confidence in learning. Often when educators reflect on projects they themselves engaged in as students, they think of dioramas, trifold boards, glue sticks, and scissors. They spent a significant amount of class time cutting, pasting, and presenting information (as opposed to reading, writing, and discussing). We probably all remember the shoebox cell structure that we presented to our peers, a few parents, and our teacher.

Today technology allows for projects that include slide decks, Prezis, podcasts, and websites. But the question we need to be asking is, "What are students thinking about as they engage in these activities?" Daniel Willingham (2009), once stated that memory is the residue of thought. If kids are pasting, scrolling, and cutting, are they thinking about the essential concepts of a discipline? Does a kid who is building a cell in a shoebox think about what happens when something atypical occurs inside of a cell? How do we ensure that students are spending time debating issues, clarifying thoughts, and challenging each other's reasoning?

Unfortunately, meaningful content learning often takes a backseat to other priorities like developing engaging products or providing engaging instruction in projects that suffer from "miss the mark" pitfalls. Mike Schmoker (2011) warns against this type of trend by critiquing certain "innovative" shifts currently being promoted.

> He is always innovating. He has initiated interdisciplinary teaching, heavy use of technology, hands-on activities, and lots of "project based learning." His students do very little reading and even less writing. But they spend lots of time going to and from the library, often preparing, making, and then listening (listlessly) to each other's flashy but unfocused PowerPoint presentations. And like the majority of the teachers at his school, he doesn't even realize that his lessons and projects are devoid of modeling, guided practice, or checks for understanding. Nonetheless, the teacher is highly regarded for his emphasis on "active" learning, on "integrating technology" into his "project based" assignments. (p. 55)

This depicts a common example of "miss the mark" pitfalls. The teacher described here is not using assessment practices to identify student progress and then, in light of that data, making clear instructional decisions that are known to substantially impact a child's learning. The teacher is spending tons of time on project management or process-oriented criteria such as completing a project; finishing tasks; and searching for, collecting, and reviewing resources. In many PBL classrooms, students are spending time building, doing, and creating resources and products in which the expectations are associated with the aesthetics of the product over learning valuable content.

Schmoker (2011) goes further, stating that organizations that advocate for project- and problem-based learning as an appropriate method for enhancing student learning also challenge the very idea of having clear learning intentions and success criteria that are anchored in core content knowledge and skills.

> One of the popular 21st century organizations is advancing a set of "standards" that would supplant meaningful reading and writing activities with having students make websites, video movie trailers, clay animation figures, wikis, sound tracks, and posters— each reflecting students' "individual personalities." These are seductive, multi-day activities that sound so much more interesting to some teachers than the authentic literacy activities they would replace. (p. 75)

In his blog *Granted, and . . . ~ thoughts on education*, Grant Wiggins (2013) reiterates Schmoker's claim that flashy projects devoid of core content often lack substance and inhibit meaningful learning.

> I saw a huge multi-day effort on Victorian culture involving dress up, tea party, Dickens characters, etc. take 2 days and 2000 dollars in a middle school and I thought it was the biggest waste of time I had ever seen. "But the kids love it!" So? It really caused no take-away learning. So until and unless you can show me how the activity meets important goals related to understanding then I am going to remain a tad skeptical.

Projects such as those described by Wiggins and Schmoker emphasize that products that lack cognitively demanding tasks (i.e., devoid of reading, writing, and talking) and lack content-rich learning intentions are not likely to have a significant impact on student achievement. In these examples, teachers have focused their conscious efforts on context-rich problems and tasks rather than on ensuring students learn core content that will enable them to apply that understanding in a variety of different contexts. Moreover, the teachers in these examples have determined that motivation is associated with focusing learners on engaging contexts and products as opposed to challenging learners in seeing discrepancies in their prior knowledge with content expectations.

If these pitfalls are typical in the project- and problem-based classroom, then it is not surprising that Hattie (2009) found that when you compare project-based learning as a method with that of other instructional approaches, the net effect on student learning is *far* less than desirable. Yes, project-based learning works to improve student achievement, but then almost everything works. How can we ensure that PBL achieves a greater effect size? Can a teacher create an engaging project and ensure core learning? Can a teacher motivate learners by providing an exciting scenario and illuminating cognitive gaps? Absolutely! And, to do so, teachers must consider a few steps in the project design process.

Voices From the Trenches

Steve Zipkes
Founder and President of Advanced Reasoning in Education, LLC
Founding Principal, Cedars International Next Generation High School
Founding Former Principal, Manor New Technology High School
Austin, TX
advancedreasoningined.com
cedars-academy.org

I have been working in PBL schools for well over 10 years. We decided to implement schoolwide project-based learning at Cedars International Next Generation High School based on the belief that the pinnacle of learning is not mastery but rather a student's ability to transfer knowledge and skills to other situations and environments. PBL is a vehicle that can effectively move students to that level of learning. In addition, PBL provides students with the opportunity to take ownership over their own learning, tackle authentic real-life problems, and collaborate with others. Our school places a premium on these outcomes.

We have observed instruction in PBL that is related to the pitfalls in the book— teachers sometimes miss the mark by not teaching the key standards; or they only scratch the surface of learning by not ensuring that students master the core content or develop the confidence to monitor their own learning. We have continued to put a vested effort in ensuring that students learn the content through appropriate scaffolding and effective teaching. We are determined to balance authentic products with rigorous understanding. Or to put it differently, blend rigor with relevance. We do this by presenting challenging problems, giving students an opportunity to engage with content, identifying their understanding, and then adapting our instruction based on their needs. I think PBL practice in the past or, frankly, done incorrectly has been related to "free will" and "exploration" with a mindset of "just figure it out."

In the end, deeper learning requires a deep understanding of content. This book, bottom line, is about kids learning content, and our efforts in Texas have shown effective results because we ensure that students learn core content and engage in creating authentic products.

The argument in this book is that three key design shifts must be specifically inscribed in the design and implementation of project-based learning. This starts with understanding that the role of the teacher requires a monumental shift. In classrooms where the pitfalls are prevalent, teachers are often found doing the work of project management: assisting students in completing tasks, managing groups, and completing products. What they should be doing is providing targeted instruction on key learning outcomes and leveraging learners as resources for each other in building student confidence. The work of teachers is to focus on children's thinking, to make that thinking visible, and to act on that thinking to move learning forward. To be effective, PBL needs to be directly anchored to thinking, to the science of learning, and to high-impact teaching practices. Over the past few decades, the method has evolved, but the alignment of teacher actions with the cognitive work of learners has not been as clearly articulated and executed in all classrooms. Teachers haven't been armed with practical strategies to enable students to be aware of and develop a command over their own learning and to use strategies that substantially build academic literacy— they are now. Figure 2.3 offers an example of how a teacher can make the shift from traditional PBL toward a PBL method that emphasizes learning outcomes and making thinking visible.

How do we ensure that we, as educators, are not merely scratching the surface of PBL or fundamentally missing the mark in enabling students to learn at high levels? The argument here is that three key shifts in project design including establishing clarity of expectations, ensuring appropriate challenge for students across learning levels, and developing a culture that cultivates confidence are needed to substantially move the needle in learning. To make a marked impact on learning, teachers need to work with students to ensure that they understand the learning intentions and success criteria of the project at surface, deep, and transfer levels as well as to ensure students are able to separate the context of the project from the learning outcomes. Moreover, teachers need to ensure that students have tasks and associated instructional support at each level of learning to meet surface, deep, and transfer demands. This requires dollops of feedback and a wealth of conversations that focus on monitoring and taking action on learning.

To make a marked impact on learning, teachers need to work with students to ensure that they understand the learning intentions and success criteria of the project at surface, deep, and transfer levels as well as to ensure students are able to separate the context of the project from the learning outcomes.

To put this work into reality, a teacher would follow a project or problem design process by initiating or introducing the transfer-level expectations upfront, and then the teacher would provide instruction to support students at their level of understanding. Figure 2.4 shows a linear progression of supporting students in learning surface- to deep- to transfer-level outcomes. For example, in the Nairobi

FIGURE 2.3 Shifting in Teacher Roles to Focus on Student Learning

TRADITIONAL PBL	UPDATED PBL
TEACHERS AS RESOURCE PERSONS	**TEACHERS AS ACTIVE INTERVENTIONISTS**
Teachers focus on gathering materials, plan activities for students to discuss the product, work with students on meeting deadlines, and engage in other administrative activities. The practices utilized are at best facilitative and at worst passive in nature.	Teachers provide direct guidance to learners based on their current level of understanding content knowledge and skill. Teachers provide instruction and feedback to students that align with their level of understanding and work with students to identify ways to improve their own learning. The practices are active in nature, constantly assessing learner understanding and adapting accordingly.
EXAMPLE	EXAMPLE
Ms. Drew continues to move around the room asking students what they need in order to complete the project. Many students are commenting on needing additional time to complete a section of a PowerPoint; others are talking about the need to change their group composition, while still others are asking for access to websites that have been blocked by administration. Often students are stuck with where to find rubrics, how to track deadlines, and schedule meetings to discuss grades. Ms. Drew works to coordinate all of these requests while reminding students of project expectations.	Ms. Drew reviews achievement data with students and asks several students to interpret the data and to devise potential next steps to enable all learners to enhance their knowledge and skills to meet project outcomes. Students decide that the entire class should create a concept map on the main ideas related to the project. Ms. Drew breaks students into groups of three to engage in a concept-mapping exercise and then meets with a few students to provide individual support in light of their performance data.

project, a teacher would typically launch the project and then provide targeted instruction and tasks at the surface level enabling students to understand carrying capacity, food chains, and food webs. Based on student performance data, teachers would need to provide different instructional support. This requires teachers to constantly ask, "What are my students thinking about during each activity?" and "What are the specific actions that I'm taking to ensure that students are advancing in their learning?"

By engaging in this process, the teacher would ensure that students who needed surface-level support would learn terms by previewing content or asking

FIGURE 2.4 Project-Based Learning Phases

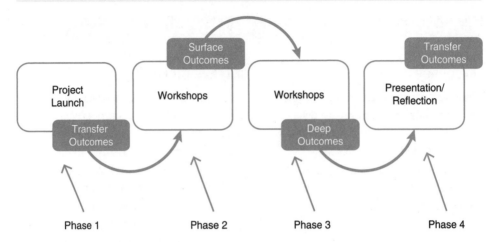

The project is considered the central teaching strategy, and students learn knowledge and skills through the project rather than outside or peripheral to the project. Projects have four key phases shown in the diagram above and described below:

Phase 1: Project Launch: Students are introduced to the transfer-level learning expectations of the project. Students are assessed on their level of understanding of surface-, deep-, and transfer-level competence.*

Phase 2: Surface Workshops: Students learn surface-level information, complete surface-level tasks, and receive instruction that is at the surface level.

Phase 3: Deeper Workshops: Students learn deeper-level information, complete deeper-level tasks, and receive instruction that is at the deeper level.

Phase 4: Presentations/Reflections: Students present their understanding of surface- and deep-level outcomes and solve transfer-level outcomes. Students also reflect on their learning.

* Based on assessment information; not all students require surface-, deep-, and transfer-level workshops.

questions that connect prior knowledge with new material. As students develop a thorough understanding of surface-level outcomes, the teacher would provide direct instruction on how to relate carrying capacities, food chains, and food webs. Next, the teacher would have students generate a plausible outcome to the presented problem and, at the same time, have the students generate a plausible solution to a problem in a different context. For example, students would solve the Nairobi National Park problem and transfer that understanding to other problems, such as how to address the Golden Eagles eradication in the Altamont Pass wind farms in Livermore, California (see Figure 2.5).

In the classroom, students will likely be in different places in their learning (i.e., some students will require surface-level knowledge while others will be

FIGURE 2.5 Project Snapshot: Altamont Pass Example

The Altamont Pass wind farm is one of the best examples of the conflicts surrounding wildlife and humans. The wind farm provides renewable energy to a carbon dependent economy. However, the farm threatens the Golden Eagles' existence due to the birds inadvertently being hit by the large turbines while hunting. The California Department of Wildlife is currently developing a proposal for closing the wind farm, which will ultimately impact the people who depend on the energy it generates. Drawing on what we know about carrying capacity, food chains, food webs, and the dynamics of environmental concerns on local communities, how would you advise the California Department of Wildlife?

prepared for deeper-level understanding). The beauty of PBL and the design elements discussed in this book is that teachers will have an arsenal of strategies to support students no matter where they are in their learning. Moreover, the design process prescribed in this text offers teachers several options to give students multiple ways to apply their skills to multiple contexts and develop students' capacity to measure their own learning.

PBL design must be advanced to ensure that miss the mark interpretations and scratch the surface practices are eliminated. Research shows that PBL does have a net impact on deeper-learning outcomes *but only* if learners know basic content well, are able to relate ideas, and are looking for opportunities to extend their learning. As Hattie (2011) states, "It is the application and principles underlying the knowledge, rather than the concepts or knowledge, that are most influenced by problem-based learning. The application of knowledge, not development of knowledge, is the heart of the success of problem-based learning" (p. 211). By implementing a few design-oriented shifts, all students will have a higher probability of learning at high levels.

PBL by design provides a clear expectation that students will apply knowledge and skills to transfer-level problems. This text argues that specific practices (clarity of expectations, challenge and intervention, instilling a culture of confidence) must be emphasized and used consistently to make a substantial impact on learning for all learners at all levels. Clarity of expectations yields an effect size of 0.75, which represents a dramatic effect on student learning. Additionally, providing challenge produces an average effect size of 0.73. Finally, developing confidence in learning has effect sizes of 0.54 and 1.44 respectively. Collectively, these strategies are arguably the most effective and efficient approaches to enhancing student learning and establishing confidence.

This book provides steps on how to design clarity of expectations of student learning in projects (Chapter 3), incorporate challenge and intervention (Chapter 4), and create a culture of confidence to prepare students for self-directed and collaborative learning (Chapter 5). Collectively, the integration of these high-impact strategies may be effectively codified and interwoven in project design to build student confidence and substantially enhance student competency.

CONCLUSION

The work for teachers and students is to home in on those actions that have a high probability of yielding high impact on learning. Though quality criteria are available, the approach can be more impactful when specific design shifts are articulated and embedded in the PBL methodology. The next several chapters provide practitioners with specific actions and examples to implement the PBL design shifts in their classroom to yield a high impact on learning and, as such, develop competent and confident learners.

QUESTIONS FOR REFLECTION

- Why are the three key design shifts critical to project design?

- What do you know now that you didn't know before reading this chapter? How does this new information inform your practice? What challenges have emerged for you—are there ideas you don't agree with? What questions do you have?

- What did you see as the key messages to share with your colleagues about PBL?

- What are some of the major challenges of PBL? What are the major strengths and opportunities of the methodology?

- How do these key design shifts impact a student's learning?

- How do you see your role in the PBL classroom?

ACTIVITIES

Review the following suggested changes to the Gold Standard characteristics and identify the potential shifts required in practice:

- **Challenging Problem or Question:** Engagement in learning is based on students recognizing the difference in their current thinking from that which is required in the project. Knowledge is gained to remember content as that knowledge builds to enable students to apply it to the current problem or project and to transfer that understanding to other situations.

- **Sustained Inquiry:** Teachers play a key role in the inquiry process and ensure learners are using inquiry to move forward in their learning. Teachers provide instruction to enable learners to enhance their learning. Teachers are constantly assessing learners and working with learners to identify the best means to support their own learning. Questions such as *Where are you going in your learning? Where are you?* and *What's next?* are common in the classroom.

- **Authenticity:** Focusing on learners' genuine discussion of their learning and how that learning relates to authentic aspects of a project, including the perspectives of others within various contexts.

- **Student Voice and Choice:** Student voice and choice is focused more squarely on their learning as opposed to the project. Learners determine how they want to investigate their progress and proficiency, how they will demonstrate what they have learned, and how they will share their work.

- **Reflection:** Learners focus on the changes in their learning and what strategies they utilized to improve their rate of progress and level of proficiency.

- **Critique and Revision:** Learners are taught how to give and receive constructive peer feedback that will improve individual and peer learning as well as products and processes.

- **Public Product:** Provides a venue to showcase the learning that occurred throughout the project.

What are the noticeable differences in the Gold Standard expectations in how they are written? How do such differences shift our thinking about project design and the specific actions teachers could take to support students in their learning?

Searching for Sample Projects

1. Go to the Buck Institute of Education website at http://bie.org/project_search or visit the YouCubed tasks at page https://www.youcubed.org/tasks.

2. Select a project or problem that is related to specific learning intentions that you are interested in having students learn.

3. Review the project and problem for the three design shifts using the table on the facing page.

4. Questions to consider asking include the following: *What evidence of the three design shifts is readily identified in each project or problem? What appears to be missing? How would you enhance the project to leverage the three design shifts?*

DESIGN SHIFT REVIEW TABLE

	DESIGN SHIFT I: CLARITY OF EXPECTATIONS	DESIGN SHIFT II: CHALLENGE AND INTERVENTION	DESIGN SHIFT III: CULTURE OF CONFIDENCE
When reviewing a project, look for . . .	• Clear learning intentions are identified in the project resources (entry event, rubric). • Success Criteria are easily identified in project resources.	• Lessons or workshops that are specific to surface-, deep-, and transfer-level learning • Lessons or workshops are aligned with and mapped to a project calendar from surface-, deep-, to transfer-level learning.	• Protocols and agreements • Tools and processes for leveraging voice and choice
When developing your own project, include . . .	• Identify key learning intentions. • Create success criteria for each outcome at surface (single ideas/skills), deep (multiple ideas/skills), and transfer (applying skills/ideas) levels. • Create questions for each outcome at surface, deep, and transfer levels. • Develop multiple tasks that align with surface, deep, and transfer levels. • Develop an entry document to show students the expectation of the project. • Provide task-specific criteria (consider a competency-based rubric).	• Structure workshops from surface to deep to transfer expectations. • Sequence workshops from surface to deep to transfer expectations. • Map key events on project calendar. • Plan for the use of the "four questions" (see Chapter 4) to drive intervention. • Utilize a need-to-know list.	• Protocols and agreements to ensure students inspect their own learning • Protocols and agreements to ensure students can make choices
When developing or reviewing a project, consider using the following questions including . . .	• What are the content goals? • What are surface-, deep-, and transfer-level expectations? • What is the context of the project? What alternative contexts are available? • Do assessments clearly articulate the expectations of learning?	• How do students meet surface-, deep-, and transfer-level expectations? • How are surface-, deep-, and transfer-level workshops aligned? • How do teachers identify student progress and proficiency?	• How do students leverage voice and choice? • How do they inspect their progress and proficiency? • How does the class as a whole give and receive feedback? • How does the class as a whole make decisions?

NEXT STEPS

- Write down what you know about the three design shifts and what you need to know. As you go through the book, identify where your prior knowledge was tested and where ideas were confirmed. Furthermore, continue to develop a list of questions or "need-to-knows" throughout the book and reflect on how those questions move from surface, to deep, and to transfer.

- With a team of teachers, review the facts (what you know) and inferences/assumptions about PBL (what you think you know based on those facts, or put another way, "What are the stories we tell ourselves about PBL?"). For example, you might say, "I know that teachers play an important role in the classroom." As for inferences/assumptions, you may get several different answers. This is a great place to discuss the assumptions you and your team operate under in PBL. Next, you can craft next steps in improving PBL design and implementation. To assist in this collaborative exercise, you may want to use Protocol 2.1, What? So What? Now What?

PROTOCOL 2.1: What? So What? Now What?

▶ The following protocol allows participants to separate observations and facts from inferences/assumptions in order to make effective individual and collective decisions.

Total Time: 35 minutes

Opening Moves (Introduction) (5 minutes)

- Review purpose of the protocol.
- Review agreements (or norms) of the team.
- Identify facilitator/participant and participants.

Statements of Problem/Challenge/Circumstance: *What?* (10 minutes)

- The facilitator asks a participant to outline a current challenge/problem/or circumstance.
- The facilitator asks for clarifying questions from other participants.
- The facilitator then asks everyone to identify the facts of the challenge/problem or circumstance. (What do we know are facts from this challenge?)
- The facilitator incorporates that information onto a chart under the term "What?"

Mastering Our Stories: *So What?* (10 minutes)

- The facilitator then asks what appear to be inferences/assumptions that are drawn from the challenge. (What are we assuming or taking for granted? What other assumptions may there be?) The facilitator incorporates this information onto a chart under the term "So What?"
- The facilitator asks the participants to consider all of the people who are impacted by this challenge and identify what assumptions they may possess in this challenge.

Taking Action: *Now What?* (10 minutes)

- Next, the facilitator asks each participant to write down three or four specific next steps on sticky notes. The facilitator provides the following prompts: "What additional information do we need?" "What assumptions do we need to check?" "What appear to be logical next steps in moving toward a solution?"
- The facilitator asks the participants to silently place their sticky notes under a column titled "Next Steps." Participants may group the sticky notes quietly.

(Continued)

- The facilitator then asks the group to describe the groupings. (What appear to be the major themes related to next steps?)

- The facilitator asks the original participant if he or she would like to share next steps being considered.

- The facilitator then asks the original participant when he or she should check back on action steps and outcomes.

- The session is then closed.

 Available for download at **us.corwin.com/rigorouspblbydesign** under the "Preview" tab

CHAPTER 3

Design Shift I: Clarity
Understanding Expectations of Learning Upfront

Teaching in the dark is a questionable practice.

—Deborah Taba & Hilda Elkins (1966)

CLEAR EXPECTATIONS MOTIVATE LEARNING

In 1996, Electronic Arts released Tetris, a video game that requires players to move a series of blocks of different shapes to fit together to form a straight line. When lines are created the entire line is deleted. After completing a series of lines, the game speeds up and players have to make quicker and quicker decisions to complete lines and not allow blocks to stack up and hit the top of the screen. Sound fun? Tetris has sold more copies than any other game ever.

Video games are incredibly addicting and Tetris is a vivid example of why: the game provides clear expectations to a player (players move blocks to make a line to win), clear progression of learning (as players gain proficiency the game becomes more difficult), clear feedback (players have an explicit display of blocks that either fit or don't fit to make a line), and multiple opportunities to master the game (players can play multiple times which allows them to "try again and try differently").

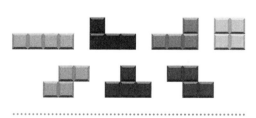

IMAGE SOURCE: Wikimedia Commons/Damian Yerrick

Video games provide answers to important questions that drive learning such as, *What are the expectations? How am I performing?* and, *What do I need to do to get better?* Think back to the 99 cent games you downloaded on your smartphone, and reflect on your motivation for such purchases. Games give people immediate feedback based on set criteria and multiple opportunities to continue to engage in the same strategy or attempt new strategies to succeed, to progress, to master. The goal of the game is readily available and transparent. These aforementioned elements are paramount for learning. For instance, clarity of expectations has been documented time and time again in the research as an important motivator for learning and as a factor that has a substantial impact on learning (Clarke, 2015).

The common characteristics that drive us to play Tetris or Angry Birds may be translated to the classroom in the following questions:

1. Where am I going in my learning?

2. Where am I now in my learning?

3. What next steps am I going to take in my learning?

4. How do I improve my learning and that of others?

Such questions shape instructional design, wherein teachers focus their efforts on providing clarity to students on learning expectations at surface, deep, and transfer levels. Moreover, instructional design enables students to gain clarity regarding their own current performance levels so they may identify next steps to reach content-based goals. Put another way, *instructional design* is about creating a plan that substantially moves a student's understanding and skill set to much higher levels through a project (or unit or lesson). To accomplish such a feat, expectations for learning must be clear, performance levels well established, and next steps that students need to take in their own learning process must be well planned. This chapter focuses on shaping project design to enable students to address Question 1, *Where am I going?* with absolute clarity.

> *Instructional design* is about creating a plan that substantially moves a student's understanding and skill set to much higher levels through a project (or unit or lesson).

WHERE AM I GOING IN MY LEARNING?

As in the previous video game example, clear expectations draw us in to learning new things. John Hattie and Gregory Donoghue (2016) argue that students who know what is expected are "more likely to be strategic in their choice of learning strategies, more likely to enjoy the thrill of success in learning, and more likely to reinvest in attaining even more success criteria" (p. 6). Possessing clarity of work expectations is well documented as a key motivational factor in business (Lencioni, 2015) and in general pop psychology (Pink, 2011); and it yields a substantial effect on student learning (Hattie, 2009). Students' ability to articulate and understand what is expected of them provides them with the ability to self-assess (Where am I now in relation to what is expected?), self-improve (What next steps should

I take?), and ask for assistance (Who can help me?), which enable learners to increase their learning and develop confidence.

One of the distinguishing attributes of problem-based learning (PBL), when designed correctly, is that clear learning intentions and success criteria are provided at the very beginning of the learning sequence (see Figure 3.1). In particular, during Phase 1 (i.e., Project Launch), teachers introduce students to the surface, deep, and transfer expectations that they will need to address during the project. By providing an overt articulation of expectations early on, students have a clear picture of *where they are going* over the next several weeks. Further, as students engage in Phase 2 and Phase 3 work, they have a clear rationale for why they are learning surface- and deep-level knowledge as it is connected to the transfer learning expectations of the project. Additionally, an indirect result of this process is that showcasing high expectations for student learning upfront sends an implicit message to children that teachers believe they can learn and learn at high levels.

FIGURE 3.1 Project-Based Learning Phases

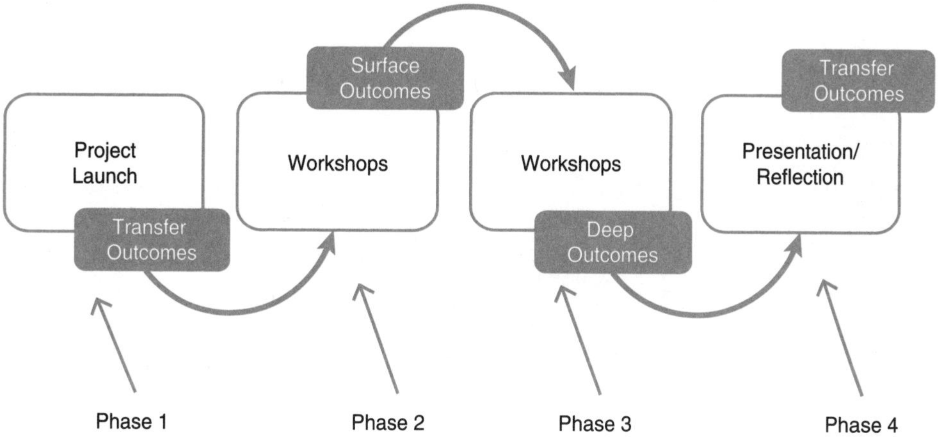

To ensure clarity, two design challenges emerge for teachers:

1. Separating context and tasks from learning intentions and success criteria

2. Scaffolding surface-, deep-, and transfer-level expectations effectively

First Design Challenge: Be Clear About Separating Context and Task From Learning Intentions and Success Criteria

In the pursuit of establishing clarity of learning intentions (i.e., goals) and success criteria (i.e., expectations to reach goals), teachers face two interesting challenges. First, projects are inherently context rich, and teachers must be able to support students in being able to separate the project situation or context from the learning intentions and success criteria. For example, in The House M.D. project (Figure 3.2), students may focus their mental effort on diagnosis, prognosis, and identifying a treatment plan for a patient at the hospital. This makes sense as the product expectations for the project are laid out in the example. However, as a teacher, I'm looking for students to understand and explain the relationship between bacteria, viruses, and protists to the immune system. The House M.D. Project is the vehicle or context to introduce the content of the immune system into my classroom. If students do not understand the learning intentions and success criteria that are in the project, they will often be unable to transfer their understanding to new contexts and situations and they will lack the surface- and deep-level understanding I want them to gain.

By consciously separating learning outcomes and success criteria from the project context, students can readily transfer their learning to various situations and articulate their understanding in various ways. Take, for example, a teacher who did the same lesson twice with two different groups of

FIGURE 3.2 Project Snapshot: The House M.D. Project

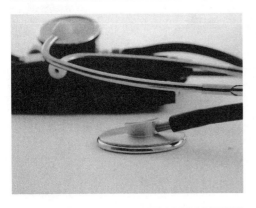

IMAGE SOURCE: Pixabay/Darko Stojanovic

In the following projects, students are provided with details on an ailing patient at a nearby hospital. The health professionals at the hospital are interested to learn about the students' ability to discern the diagnosis, craft a treatment plan, and identify a prognosis. The health professions will be attending a special presentation in a few short weeks to understand how students applied the cell biology, microbiology, and immunology to address the needs of the patient.

► **Key Questions**

As you read the initial description of the project, think about the following questions:

- What are the key learning intentions of the project?
- What are the success criteria of the project at the surface, deep, and transfer levels?

After reflecting on the aforementioned questions, review and engage in Activity 3.7 at the end of the chapter.

students. For the first group, the teacher introduced the learning outcome with the context embedded (they were asked to write the story of Goldilocks from a different perspective). For the second group, the teacher provided students with the decontextualized learning objective and then provided them with the context (they were asked to write a traditional tale from a different perspective). Interestingly, the kids in the classroom with the decontextualized outcome understood what was expected, and the kids in the classroom with the contextualized outcome fixated on the elements of Goldilocks. They were sidetracked on the context rather than the expected learning outcomes. Figure 3.3 lays out Dylan Wiliam's (2011) example of a learning outcome, context, and a confused learning objective.

> By consciously separating learning outcomes and success criteria from the project context, students can readily transfer their learning to various situations and articulate their understanding in various ways.

As shown, learning intentions and success criteria can get muddled and blend contexts, confusing students and teachers in clarifying goals and expectations. Clarity may also be impacted by including tasks within learning intentions and success criteria. As Shirley Clarke (2008) argues, "they [pupils] over-focus on the most concrete element and their thinking and talking is more likely to be about what they are doing rather than what they are learning (p. 87)." In Figure 3.4, students are expected to write a persuasive essay on perspective. The key learning intentions are related to perspective and understanding assumptions. The success criteria include defining, relating, and applying perspective and assumptions held within perspective to various contexts. An essay is one way (out of many) to convey understanding of this learning intention. The point is that learning intentions and success criteria should be indifferent to the task and the context. Students should have the opportunity to demonstrate their understanding in multiple ways (i.e., different tasks) across multiple situations (i.e., different contexts). It is important to note that if the learning intention was to write a persuasive essay, then it makes sense to develop success criteria related to writing an

FIGURE 3.3 Separating Learning Outcomes From Context

LEARNING OUTCOME	Present an argument either for or against an emotionally charged proposition.
CONTEXT	Assisted suicide
CONFUSED LEARNING OBJECTIVE	Present an argument for or against assisted suicide.

SOURCE: Used with permission. Adapted from *Embedded Formative Assessment* by Dylan Wiliam. Copyright 2011 by Solution Tree Press, 555 North Morton Street, Bloomington, IN 47404, 800.733.6786, SolutionTree.com. All rights reserved.

In the following projects, learners are expected to write a persuasive essay on the critical importance of perspective and understanding assumptions to gain clarity and empathy for others and to understand the implications of how inferences, claims, and perspective, if left unchecked, can form actions that have unintended consequences. Learners begin by reading *Beowulf* and Grendel and excerpts from various pieces on the immigration of people from the Middle East and Africa to Europe and the United States. Learners are then expected to determine how perspective, assumptions, and claims shape individual, community, and international decision making.

▶ **Key Questions**

As you read the initial description of the project, think about the following questions:

- What are the key learning intentions of the project?

- What are the success criteria of the project at the surface, deep, and transfer levels?

- What other contexts could be used to meet the learning intentions and success criteria of the project?

After reflecting on the aforementioned questions, review and engage in Activity 3.8 at the end of the chapter.

essay. In summary, our main aim is to ensure that students have a clear sense of learning intentions and success criteria. As we will see in Chapter 5, giving students a choice of various tasks enables a richer dialogue between students, teachers, and peers in determining the most effective ways to demonstrate understanding.

Second Design Challenge: Scaffold Surface-, Deep-, and Transfer-Level Expectations Effectively

The second design challenge is related to carefully scaffolding the levels of complexity necessary for students to meet the transfer-level demands of project questions and tasks. In the PBL classroom, students must be introduced to learning intentions and success criteria at surface-, deep-, and transfer-level expectations. Specifically, this text recommends building success criteria at specific levels of learning in the following way: surface learning (single and multiple ideas and skills), deep learning (combining or linking ideas and skills), and transfer learning (extending ideas and skills). Figure 3.5 illustrates these levels of learning.

FIGURE 3.5 Surface-, Deep-, and Transfer-Level Learning Rhetoric

BUILD KNOWLEDGE		MAKE MEANING	APPLY UNDERSTANDING
SINGLE (One Concept, Idea, Skill)	MULTIPLE (More Than One Concept, Idea, Skill)	LINK (Connect Concepts, Ideas, Skills)	EXTEND (Transfer Concepts, Ideas, Skills)
• Name • Tell • Restate • Define • Describe who, what, where, when, or how • Identify • Recall • Recite • Recognize • Label • Locate • Match • Measure • Solve one-step task • Use rules	• List several elements • Describe and explain using context • Classify • Give examples and nonexamples • Perform a procedure • Summarize • Estimate • Use models to perform procedure • Construct simple model • Solve multiple-step problem	• Cite supporting evidence • Organize • Outline • Interpret • Revise for meaning • Explain connections or procedures • Compare • Contrast • Synthesize • Verify • Show cause and effect • Critique • Analyze • Argue • Assess • Deconstruct • Draw conclusions • Extend patterns • Infer • Predict • Solve nonroutine problems	• Reorganize into new structure • Formulate • Generalize • Produce and present • Design and conduct • Collaborate • Evaluate • Hypothesize • Initiate • Reflect • Research

SOURCE: Based on personal communication with Larry Ainsworth, May 4, 2016.

Voices From the Trenches

Teresa Rensch
Director of Curriculum and Instruction
Konocti Unified School District, Lower Lake, CA
http://kec.konoctiusd.org

Konocti Education Center (a 4th–12th grade school) has had two years of full implementation as a health magnet, visual arts, and PBL school. Konocti Education Center landed on PBL to bring an alternative instructional method in hopes of raising

(Continued)

(Continued)

the level of relevance of school for a particular set of students in fostering 21st century capable learners. Whether a school or district, when attempting full-scale implementation, I recommend partnering with Corwin to build a viable strategic plan. Corwin can support an effective professional development plan that allows staff to

- gain new, research-informed knowledge;
- have time to make meaning of the new learning and construct the new learning for the classroom;
- receive ongoing coaching support; and
- ultimately build capacity within one's own system.

The partnership includes large-scale needs assessment and guidance in interpreting the data to narrow the focus and initial action steps that will affect student learning.

As director, I spent my first year in the school gaining knowledge through observing classes. In year two, we now make an effort to include students in reflection around their academic progress at incremental junctures in the PBL unit. There has been a shift to include more frequent formal and informal formative assessments. This supports teacher clarity around the students' levels of learning along the way. It also supports the students' awareness of their own learning progression. One thing that stands out about this school is the collaborative spirit involved in creating the schoolwide PBL units. I particularly appreciate the reflective piece at the end of the schoolwide PBL unit in which the school professional learning community (PLC) evaluates the success of the unit.

If I were leading a new school initiative to implement PBL, I would include malleable steps with clear benchmarks at each phase of the implementation plan. I would incorporate the reflection component and data analysis as part of the implementation plan. I would ensure key instructional strategies, like teacher clarity, were interwoven into the PBL units. Moving forward, we will continue to include John Hattie's research into the methodology of PBL. The school collaborative teams will include regular intervals of data analysis and progress monitoring around the effectiveness in the delivery of PBL units and lessons.

In this book, Michael McDowell provides a practical application manual for effective implementation of PBL. When I say "effective," I mean the hinge point of visible learning. McDowell delivers substantial research supporting each shift in PBL design. This book is premised on the realization that students start each PBL unit in the learning pit, and then the journey begins through the intentional arrangement of instruction, intervention, and feedback. Through implementation of these three shifts, students cross the finish line at the end each PBL unit out of the pit, at a stage of illumination and discovery, at a stage of deep and sustainable learning.

As stated earlier, PBL has a relatively low effect on student achievement at the surface level whereas PBL has shown substantial yields when students are prepared for transfer-level work. To alleviate the deficit of the method in ensuring students have developed surface knowledge and skill and to maintain the method's positive yield in supporting students in transferring core content and skills across various situations, this chapter supports teachers in designing step-by-step projects that enable students

- to have clarity of the learning intentions and success criteria at surface, deep, and transfer levels of learning, and

- to separate the learning intentions and success criteria from contexts and tasks.

STEPS FOR DETERMINING CLEAR LEARNING INTENTIONS AND SUCCESS CRITERIA IN PROJECT DESIGN

The remaining portion of this chapter walks teachers through recommended steps to ensure students can answer the question, *Where am I going in my learning?* Recommended steps include the following:

- Step 1: Prioritize key learning intentions.

- Step 2: Create success criteria at surface, deep, and transfer levels.

- Step 3: Design driving questions that align with learning intentions and success criteria and identify contexts.

- Step 4: Develop multiple tasks that align with surface, deep, and transfer learning levels.

- Step 5: Develop an entry event to orient learners to learning intentions and success criteria.

To assist in integrating all of these steps, a sample template for designing a project is offered in Figure 3.6. To find examples of projects that possess the clarity needed to substantially impact student learning, please visit Appendix B of this book. This chapter provides a brief summary of selected project samples on the following pages.

Step 1: Prioritize Key Learning Intentions

Learning intentions are best thought of as brief statements that explicitly describe what students should know (i.e., content) and be able to do (i.e., skill). These brief statements anchor all other steps in project design and serve as the focal point or "end in mind" for teachers and students to

FIGURE 3.6 Project Design Template (Abbreviated)

PROJECT DESIGN		
STEP 1: Learning Intention(s)		
STEP 2: Success Criteria		
Surface	Deep	Transfer
STEP 3: Driving Question(s)		
Context		
STEP 4: Tasks		
Surface	Deep	Transfer
STEP 5: Entry Event		
Scenario . . .		
Expectations . . .		
Patron . . .		
Format . . .		

continually refer to during projects. To determine key learning intentions, this text recommends that teachers prioritize essential standards that are deemed necessary for students to learn at the surface, deep, and transfer levels.

In most state curricular documents, there are too many learning intentions for students to cover within an academic year (Popham, 2011). In fact, Robert Marzano (Scherer, 2001, p. 15) stated, "To cover all of this content, you would have to change schooling from K–12 to K–22. . . . The sheer number of standards is the biggest impediment to implementing standards." Beyond coverage, students need multiple exposures to concepts and spaced practice to understand, relate, and extend or transfer their understanding of content and skills (Nuthall, 2007). Thus, teachers need to prioritize those standards or learning intentions that are critical for children to know and be able to do. Figure 3.7 provides a series of questions intended to help you determine those intentions that all students must know at a surface, deep, and transfer level.

FIGURE 3.7 Determining Quality Learning Intentions

How do I determine a quality learning intention?

- Will the outcome provide students with knowledge and skills beyond a test date?

- Will the learning outcomes provide knowledge and skills that are of value in multiple disciplines?

- Will the learning intention(s) provide the essential skills that are necessary for success at the next grade level?

- Will students address content that is aligned with state standards and is considered important to local and global stakeholders and communities?

- Do students have the prerequisite knowledge to meet the challenges?

- Will the learning outcome reemerge in subsequent units and courses?

- Does the knowledge and/or skill base require a level of understanding that is typically inferred in expository and narrative texts?

PROJECT 1: Whose Bug Is It Anyway?

Level: Kindergarten

Subject: Science

The following project covers several interdependent Next Generation Science Standards (California) related to Ecosystems: Animals, Plants, and Their Environment in kindergarten. In this project, Kindergarteners are being asked their opinion on whether local gardeners should introduce invasive species as a means of protecting gardens from pests. Students spend a significant amount of time understanding the similarities and differences among animals, plants, and their environment as they relate to energy consumption. Students also explore human interactions with the environment and how such interactions dramatically influence local and global environments. Students have targeted surface-, deep-, and transfer-level tasks and **workshops** that enable them to build a solid foundation of scientific understanding. The conclusion of the project has students explore overfishing and how such human actions disrupt energy consumption. The new context focuses on the relationships of animals, plants, environments, and humans; but it also provides a new perspective on intentionally removing species from an environment rather than introducing a new species to an environment.

PROJECT 2: Ratios, Rates, and Real Estate Oh My . . .

Level: Sixth Grade

Subject: Mathematics

This project focuses on understanding and applying unit rates (comparing a quantity to one unit of another quantity) to common practices in society. Students are expected to understand rates (ratios of two quantities with different units) and how to calculate rates (e.g., unit pricing and constant speed). This project requires students to use their knowledge and application of rates in the world of real estate and specifically how absorption rates impact various communities by influencing short-term and long-term appraisals. The project concludes with a one-day problem on applying the same math content in a different context. For instance, the project asks student to identify the absorption rates of different brands of paper towels and how such information may impact consumer decision making.

PROJECT 3: Changing or Maintaining Our Imperialist Imperative

Level: High School

Subject: Social Studies and English Language Arts

The following project focuses students on understanding the significant impact of industrialized nations on developing nations. The project focuses on military, social, and economic reasons for industrialized nations to interact and fundamentally influence other nations—and on the positive and negative impacts those relationships have on both parties. The project offers students the opportunity to look at contemporary issues. First, students are faced with understanding the role of the United States in the development of and maintenance of ISIS and how to face growing local and global concerns of such a development. Students develop a thorough understanding of imperialism by looking at historical patterns and analyzing causes, characteristics, and effects of European imperialism and how such patterns reflect contemporary behavior. At the conclusion of the project, students look at emerging countries and their spread of imperialism to other nations (e.g., China on Taiwan) and what role the United States should play in an omnipresent global community.

PROJECT 4: Fables, Futures, and Forecasts

Level: Third Grade

Subject: English Language Arts

The following project requires students in the third grade to develop their skills in writing by developing an opinion piece that includes a point of view with a clear rationale. To receive full marks on the final product, the students must convey their ideas clearly and must provide thorough and accurate evidence that supports their opinion. To be effective, the implementation of the project must specifically focus on the targeted skill sets while using students' knowledge gained in previous years to ensure that they are concentrating on learning new writing techniques rather than focusing on the unfamiliar context. In the second grade, students spent significant time recounting stories including fables and folktales from diverse cultures and spent time determining their central message, lessons, or morals. This project relies on the students' background knowledge of this genre of literature.

The conclusion of the project has students conduct an author's speak where students present their writing to a group of parents, community members, teachers, and peers. The presentation includes a series of questions and answers in which the students must discuss how they conducted their research and reached a point of view. After the presentations, the teacher tasks students with writing a brief opinion piece on other subjects of interest that are linked to the students' prior knowledge.

During this step, teachers should focus only on the knowledge and skills they expect students to learn and not include any tasks or products in the learning intention description. Products or tasks are the means by which students display their understanding of learning intentions. By focusing on content and skills, teachers and students allow themselves flexibility on determining how to demonstrate learning. The point here is that the learning intention should focus on the key understanding of skill and not specifically on the way to demonstrate that understanding. There are, however, certain subjects, such as English, where learning intentions that are focused on how to complete a task inherent to the subject. For example, if students are required to learn to write a persuasive text, then the learning intention should simply be "We are learning to write a persuasive text." Figure 3.8 provides examples of learning intentions across various grade levels.

FIGURE 3.8 Learning Intention Examples Across Grade Levels

Learning Intention Examples

- **Kindergarten:** I can tell others why plants and animals change their environment to survive.

- **Sixth Grade:** I can apply cause and effect in my writing.

- **Ninth Grade:** I can identify potential outcomes of protein synthesis if the flow of information from transcription of ribonucleic acid (RNA) in the nucleus to translation of proteins on ribosomes gets disrupted.

Step 2: Create Success Criteria at Surface (Single Ideas/Skills), Deep (Multiple Ideas/Skills), and Transfer (Applying Ideas/Skills) Levels

Success criteria specify what students must demonstrate at the surface, deep, and transfer level to ultimately meet learning intentions. Learning intentions cannot be met without satisfying surface-, deep-, and transfer-level understanding or skill expectations. Akin to a well-balanced meal, learners must have a balanced knowledge and skill base. One cannot survive only on protein or grains; one must have a well-balanced diet to promote healthy living and to have the opportunity to engage in the physical, cognitive, and emotional aspects of life. Learners must have the same; they must understand the basics of a subject, relationships, and principles, and how to apply such detail and content to real-world applications (within and between disciplines).

Similar to learning intentions, established success criteria are void of specifying products or tasks and instead indicate what success looks like across any task or product. Moreover, success criteria are independent of any context or situation and instead indicate what success looks like across situations. As discussed earlier, students who can discuss what is expected of them have a greater chance to identify their own performance level in relation to those outcomes and make decisions on next steps in their own learning. To design success criteria, teachers arrange the concepts and skills of the learning intention into the categories of surface, deep, and transfer (see Figure 3.9).

FIGURE 3.9 Surface, Deep, and Transfer Success Criteria Categories

Surface: Students understand single and multiple facts, details, and basic skills. Students ask, *What are the ideas that I need to know for the learning intention? What are the skills that I need to know for this learning intention?*

Deep: The second category is related to the linkage or relationships between ideas and skills that students are required to understand or apply. Students ask, *What are similarities and differences between the ideas? How do I relate skills? What connects together and what appears to be in direct contrast? Are there* *ideas that somewhat relate? How so? Are there recurring ideas, skills, or events that make up principles or main ideas in the subject?*

Transfer: Finally, the third category is related to the extension of the relationships of ideas to other contexts ("deep"). Students ask, *What are ways to apply the ideas and relationships between ideas to outside contexts? How do I apply these skills to a new task or environment?*

Let's take a look at an example of a learning intention and success criteria that define the expectation levels for students. Figure 3.10 illustrates a learning intention and success criteria that show a student is expected to understand, relate, and apply knowledge about how proteins are made and used in living organisms. At the surface level, students would need to understand specific concepts related to proteins (transcription, translation, RNA). Once a level of proficiency was developed, students would move to deeper-level learning by relating core concepts to one another (transcription and translation) and then transferring that understanding to real-life situations (internal and external influences that may impact protein creation). When students understand what is expected at the surface level (such as defining *transcription, translation, RNA*), deep level (relating concepts such as how transcription and translation are related), and transfer level (extending relationships to external contexts), they have a clear sense of expectations and can plan accordingly (as can teachers!).

Once more, keep in mind that learning intentions and success criteria are void of task-specific requirements (i.e., no assignments, project products, etc. are described) and contexts (i.e., project situations are not described in the

FIGURE 3.10 Learning Intentions and Success Criteria

PROJECT DESIGN		
STEP 1: Learning Intention(s)		
I can identify potential outcomes of protein synthesis if the flow of information from transcription of ribonucleic acid (RNA) in the nucleus to translation of proteins on ribosomes gets disrupted.		
STEP 2: Success Criteria		
Surface	Deep	Transfer
• Defines transcriptions, translation, RNA, protein	• Relates transcription and translation	• Predicts how various factors may influence protein creation

success criteria). Also worth repeating is that success criteria are directly aligned with very specific levels of learning complexity (surface, deep, and transfer). This step is critical in PBL as students face all levels of surface, deep, and transfer expectations on the first day of class when they receive their entry event. We must assist them in having as much clarity as possible!

Step 3: Design Driving Questions That Align With Learning Intentions and Success Criteria and Identify Contexts

Students are driven or pulled through the project phases by a driving question that is centered on established learning intentions and success criteria. The power of the driving question is that it provides a rationale for students of why they need to know specific learning intentions at surface, deep, and transfer levels. Moreover, the driving question places students into a certain situation or context that enables them to see the core purpose of the learning intention outside of a classroom. As such, driving questions have two key parts: (1) the learning intention and (2) the specific context in which students are expected to develop surface- and deep-level understanding to apply the learning intention. Figure 3.11 illustrates the two key parts of a driving question.

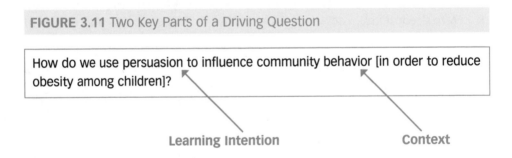

FIGURE 3.11 Two Key Parts of a Driving Question

How do we use persuasion to influence community behavior [in order to reduce obesity among children]?

Learning Intention   **Context**

Stated differently, the driving question enables students to understand *why* they are engaging in learning certain content at surface, deep, and transfer levels. As John Larmer and John Mergendoller (2010b) state, "A project without a Driving Question is like an essay without a thesis. Without one, a reader might be able to pick out the main point a writer is trying to make, but with a thesis the main point is unmistakable" (p. 37). The driving question is critically important as it serves the teacher and the students in identifying certain activities and tasks that will enable students to understand key learning intentions, meet success criteria, and take action on a contemporary challenge.

To think about it in yet another way, as we have explored, projects have four key phases: Project Launch, Surface Workshops, Deeper Workshops and Presentations and Reflections (see Figure 3.1). The driving question serves as the overall expectation (Phase 1) for students to understand the reason for learning surface- (Phase 2) and deeper-level knowledge and skills (Phase 3) to ultimately progress toward and meet the application-level knowledge and skill thus mastering the learning intentions (Phase 4). Students move from Phase 1 to Phase 4 as they develop content knowledge and skills to answer the driving questions. Throughout this process, students accomplish a multitude of tasks and understand that the context that they are encountering in the project is but one of many. As will be discussed in the next chapter, teachers use formative assessment practices and specific targeted instructional practices and means of feedback that align with surface, deep, and transfer levels of understanding and performance to ensure students are progressing at a substantial rate.

Because we are introducing context in the design process, driving questions need to be carefully constructed to ensure clarity of expectations for students. Specifically, we want students to have clarity of the learning intentions, and to understand that stated learning intentions apply in multiple contexts or situations and that the context students encounter within the driving question is but one of many. Let's look at the example in Figure 3.12 on the next page where students are asked to understand and apply the concept of imperialism to contemporary society (see Project 3 in Appendix B). The teacher has identified a learning intention, mapped out the success criteria, and has developed the following driving question: *How do the United States and other industrialized imperial nations prevent the creation of new global enemies?* It is important to point out that at this point the driving question is context neutral. As you can see, the driving question does not, for example, specifically ask why ISIS might be gaining an increasing amount of new sympathizers and supporters. However, a context (e.g., ISIS) has been identified in brackets to illustrate a context that could be used in the project. Figure 3.12 also indicates several contexts that could be used to place students in a situation in which the driving question is relevant.

To recap, when designing driving questions, keep the following points in mind:

1. **Driving questions need to specify learning intentions and the context:** Driving questions orient students to specific academic goals of the discipline(s) and a particular situation or context. Please remember that the overall aim of our work in learning is for students to transfer their surface and deep understanding to multiple situations, and thus it is critical that students can readily contrast the learning intentions and success criteria from the project context.

2. **Driving questions evoke transfer expectations:** Driving questions aim at the higher-order learning expectations and thus require teachers to support students in understanding the surface and deep success criteria required to meet such expectations.

FIGURE 3.12 Sample Intentions, Criteria, and Driving Question

PROJECT DESIGN		
STEP 1: Learning Intention(s)		
To understand that industrialized nations' desire for abundant resources and new markets for their goods, coupled with feelings of cultural superiority and increased military power, allowed for and encouraged imperial expansion.		
STEP 2: Success Criteria		
Surface	Deep	Transfer
• The student lists political, economic, and social reasons that drove 19th century European countries to take over other nations.	• The student relates the causes, characteristics, and effects of 19th century European imperialism, making evaluations of specific countries' imperialistic actions.	• The student evaluates the present day legacy of imperialism in at least one region of the world. • The student makes a hypothesis on the impact imperialism has in various contemporary contexts.

STEP 3: Driving Question(s)
How do the United States and other industrialized imperial nations prevent the creation of new global enemies? [developing the next ISIS]

Context

• ISIS

• Global trade

• Economic sanctions

                                  Learning Intention   **Context**

To adhere to these points when drafting driving questions, the following two substeps are recommended:

A. Design content- and skill-specific questions

B. Develop contexts

By taking the time to follow the two substeps of designing content-specific questions and developing contexts, you will ensure that your learners understand the learning intentions and success criteria.

Substep A: Design Content- and Skill-Specific Questions

When designing content- and skill-specific questions, keep in mind that questions should be independent of any specific situations or tasks so that students may focus on the content and skills that may be transferred to multiple situations. For example, in Figure 3.13, the teacher reviewed the learning intention and success criteria and developed discipline-specific questions at the surface, deep, and transfer level. You may notice that the transfer-level question represents the learning intention aspect of the driving question.

FIGURE 3.13 Key Discipline-Specific Questions

PROJECT DESIGN		
Surface	Deep	Transfer
• What is *translation*? What is *transcription*? What is *RNA*?	• How are proteins made through the transcription and translation process?	• How can changes in the protein synthesis process alter protein development?

Substep B: Develop Contexts

The next step is for teachers to generate several situations or contexts that are relevant to the learning intention aspect of the driving question. One suggested approach is to brainstorm several options and build as many scenarios as possible and field-test them with students, peers, or anyone who will listen. As an illustration of developing a number of contexts, a teacher who crafted the discipline-centered questions in Figure 3.13 would be interested in situations where protein synthesis is important. For example, the teacher may brainstorm topics such as cancer, GMOs, or HIV. Next, the teacher would connect the possible contexts to the discipline-centered questions within Figure 3.13. Figure 3.14 provides a specific example of connecting a science learning intention with a list of contextual examples.

FIGURE 3.14 Possible Contexts and Driving Questions

OUTCOME EXPECTATIONS	DRIVING QUESTIONS
Extended: *context I* **HIV**	How can changes in the protein synthesis process alter protein development?
Extended: *context II* **cancer**	How can changes in the protein synthesis process alter protein development?
Extended: *context III* **GMO**	How can changes in the protein synthesis process alter protein development [and impact local food production]?

Once you have connected the learning intention and context to a question, this text recommends that you analyze the degree to which your driving question is provocative, relatable to students, answerable, and clear. Figure 3.15 provides a quality driving-question checklist that may assist you in developing questions.

In summary, a quality driving question articulates the learning or academic expectations students must obtain and the context of the project. When the driving question is presented to students, it is paramount that the teacher support students in separating the learning intentions and context and that the teacher break down the learning intentions into the necessary surface, deep, and transfer success criteria.

Step 4: Develop Multiple Tasks That Align With Surface-, Deep-, and Transfer-Level Learning

Once learning intentions, success criteria, and a driving question have been developed, a wealth of tasks should be created and aligned with surface, deep, and transfer success criteria. Instead of defining one type of task for all students to complete, this text suggests that a broader array of tasks and assessment types be created to enable teachers and students to have choice in ways to convey understanding. Simultaneously, teachers should ensure that the majority of tasks include plenty of opportunities for students to read, write, and talk.

In *PBL in the Elementary Grades: Step-by-Step Guidance Tools and Tips for Standards-Focused K–5 Products* (2014), Sara Hallermann, John Larmer, and John Mergendoller advocate for engaging students in authentic

FIGURE 3.15 Quality Driving-Question Checklist

USING THE FOLLOWING DESCRIPTORS AND THE SCALE OF 1–4, HOW WOULD YOU RATE YOUR DRIVING QUESTION?				
Provocative: Questions are emotionally charged, designed to evoke emotion, a call to action	1	2	3	4
• **Initial (1–2):** How do the beliefs of people influence and impact the rights of others?				
• **Emerging (3–4):** How do conservative policies influence women's rights related to abortion?				
Answerable: Questions are able to be addressed by students and staff	1	2	3	4
• **Initial (1–2):** How has technology affected world history?				
• **Emerging (3–4):** Does technology make war more or less humane?				
Relational	1	2	3	4
• **Initial (1–2):** How does the author use tone and diction in *The Walk in the Woods*?				
• **Emerging (3–4):** How do we convey our experience of travel with others?				
Academic and Applicable	1	2	3	4
• **Initial (1–2):** How can changes in the protein synthesis process alter protein development? What treatments enhance patient survival rates with HIV?				
• **Emerging (3–4):** What, if any, antiviral drug treatments increase and maintain normal protein development in patients with HIV over time? Explain the most effective strategy to date.				
Concrete and Challenging	1	2	3	4
• **Initial (1–2):** How do architects use geometry?				
• **Emerging (3–4):** How can we design a theater that meets specifications with the greatest number of seats?				
Other	1	2	3	4

SOURCE: Questions derived from Markham, Larmer, & Ravitz (2003).

 Available for download at **us.corwin.com/rigorouspblbydesign** under the "Preview" tab

products that mirror the tasks that experts in professional organizations engage in as part of their vocation. For example, students may play the role of a public health official while developing and designing an informational brochure to educate the community about the Zika virus. Whenever possible, we'd like to see students engage in the work of experts. However, experts and novices have striking differences, including the level of prior knowledge and skill due to their level of education, encounters with others in the field, and direct exposure in the field, which fundamentally shape the way they think. Experts have spent significant time consciously focusing their efforts on their discipline and have received corrective feedback for years on their understanding of surface- and deep-level understanding. Over time, such experts have developed a way of organizing their understanding that frees up working memory to see deeper relationships among ideas, discern relevant from irrelevant information, and make calculated estimations to solutions that are close approximations to desired solutions. Experts have the opportunity to create new knowledge and are skilled at developing products in their field such as business plans (company CEO), menus (chef), plans for land use (city planner), or a medical brochure that embeds deep understanding of content (public health organizer).

Students however are novices lacking the background knowledge, practice, and time to organize the information required to engage in authentic products. Students should not be spending excessive amounts of time thinking about developing and presenting products, but rather thinking about the content and skills embedded within the product. Students *need* to focus their time and effort on thinking deeply about the disciplines of business, culinary arts, civics, and biology before they create a product that honors the expertise of a profession. One way to do this is to focus student learning on *reading, writing,* and *talking.* As discussed by Mike Schmoker (2011), cognitive activities such as reading, writing, and talking enable students to build core competencies resulting in surface-, deep-, and transfer-level understanding and skill.

Could you have students create an authentic product? Yes, but this should be underscored by authentic cognitive tasks that orient the mind to the conscious effort required to understand content and skills. As Daniel Willingham (2009) states, "Cognition early in training is fundamentally different from cognition late in training" (p. 127). Focus students *more* on the content and *less* on the product. To support teachers in this effort, Figure 3.16 illustrates an example of surface, deep, and transfer tasks that require students to read, write, and talk about learning intentions and success criteria related to imperialism.

As a next step, teachers should organize reading, writing, and talking tasks to surface-, deep-, and transfer-level success criteria (see Figure 3.17).

Once tasks have been selected, teachers may want to create a brief checklist for students to know what needs to be completed to satisfy the task requirements. Checklists may be developed by the teacher, coconstructed with the class, or in some cases, developed by the student. As stated earlier, tasks are means for achieving and demonstrating understanding surface, deep, and transfer expectations of established learning intentions. As an example, if students need to craft a literature review, then teachers should develop a clear list of criteria to be successful in meeting the task (e.g., APA in-text citations, a thesis statement that clarifies the specific areas being reviewed). A sample task checklist is shown in Figure 3.18.

FIGURE 3.16 Project Example (also see Project 3 in Appendix B): Project Design

PROJECT DESIGN		
STEP 1: Learning Intention(s)		
The industrialized nations' desire for abundant resources and new markets for their goods, coupled with feelings of cultural superiority (such as Social Darwinism) and increased military power, allowed for and encouraged imperial expansion. Imperialism had lasting positive and negative effects.		
STEP 2: Success Criteria		
Surface	Deep	Transfer
• The student lists political, economic, and social reasons that drove 19th century European imperialism.	• The student relates the causes, characteristics, and effects of 19th century European imperialism, making evaluations of specific countries' imperialistic actions.	• The student evaluates the present day legacy of imperialism in at least one region of the world. • The student makes a hypothesis on the impact imperialism has in various contemporary contexts.

(Continued)

FIGURE 3.16 (Continued)

STEP 3: Driving Question(s)		
How do the United States and other industrialized imperial nations prevent creating new global enemies?		
Context • ISIS • Global trade • Economic sanctions		

STEP 4: Tasks		
Surface	Deep	Transfer
Address the following in pairs and with the class: • Identify conditions of imperialism. • Define terms and concepts of Social Darwinism, patriarchy, and capitalism. • Identify types and sources of power: political, economic, religious, and ideological.	Using case study material for 19th century United States, European, Middle Eastern, African, and Asian nations, build a graphic organizer that • identifies which nations had power and what type. • identifies the basis for the types of powers listed above. • explains how that power was exercised. • determines what impact imperialistic nations had on each nation. • identifies the conditions that existed in each nation that either resulted in its becoming a dominant or dominated nation.	• Develop a white paper on the best solution for the United States and Allied forces to employ to ensure the safety and security of the people around the world by defeating groups such as ISIS. • Present three actions the United States and Allied nations can take to mitigate risk to citizens while building positive relations with previously imperialized regions of the world.

FIGURE 3.17 Sample Assessment Options in Literacy

CRITERIA	SAMPLE ASSESSMENTS
Surface	**Reading:** Preview a passage and highlight key ideas.
	Writing: List and describe key ideas.
	Talking: Recite key ideas.
Deep	**Reading:** Place annotations when key inferences about relationships and principles become apparent.
	Writing: Construct a thesis statement that depicts the relationships of key ideas.
	Talking: Argue the key principles and inferences from a passage.
Transfer	**Reading:** Find other texts that draw on similar inferences and principles within a different context.
	Writing: Write an opinion piece.
	Talking: Argue how the key principles and inferences from the class-based passage relate to a new context in front of a panel.

FIGURE 3.18 Task Checklist

Your literature review must include the following:

- A thesis
- APA citations
- Primary sources
- Garamond 12-point font
- Double-spaced
- Research relevant to learning intentions and success criteria
- Limitations in the research

Step 5: Develop an Entry Event to Orient Learners to Learning Intentions and Success Criteria

The final step of ensuring clarity of learning expectations and success criteria for students is to develop an entry event. As stated earlier, PBL introduces clear learning intentions and success criteria at the beginning of the learning sequence. In particular, during Phase 1 (i.e., Project Launch) teachers introduce students to the surface, deep, and transfer expectations that they will need to address during the project. By providing an overt articulation of expectations early on, students have a clear picture of *where they are going* over the next several weeks. The entry event serves as a way to launch the learning sequence and provide students with the critical information they need to move from surface- to deep- to transfer-level learning. Specifically, the entry event introduces the learning intentions and success criteria, driving question, the context of the problem, and task expectations. The entry event is typically written by the patron who is requesting assistance in answering the driving question. Figure 3.19 provides an example of an entry event for a kindergarten class.

FIGURE 3.19 Entry Event Example

Getting to know you!

Welcome to our school! We are so excited to have you here! Our school is developing a brief description of each student so that teachers, parents, the friendly reptile in the science class, and your friends (in all classes) know who you are.

We would like you to write sentences with pictures that tell us who you are, as letters (text) and picture (illustrations) are a good way to describe who you are. I also want you to be prepared to answer the following question: *How do illustrations and texts help people understand you and others?* Our presentations will happen October 20th. Let me know if you have any questions. We are looking forward to learning more about you!

Kind regards,

Principal

Labels: Scenario, Expectations, Driving Question, Patron

Entry events can come in any form imaginable including

- adult expert presentations,
- documents,
- podcasts, and
- film.

Quality entry events embed specific information that directs students to inquire about surface, deep, and transfer outcomes. Project designers refer to this embedded information as "breadcrumbs" after the classic story of Hansel and Gretel, where the children laid out breadcrumbs so they could find their way home. Project designers embed these clues through written, auditory, or visual ways to elicit questions and to frame future discussions, instructions, and assessments. To craft such an event, teachers may want to list the key components of an entry event in a blank template. For examples of filled-in templates, see Figure 3.20 and Figure 3.22. Figure 3.21 provides a description of each criterion.

Figure 3.23 illustrates how the five steps come together to enable students and teachers to have absolute clarity during the learning sequence. Figure 3.24 provides a sample entry event for the project.

FIGURE 3.20 Entry Event Criteria Example 1

ENTRY EVENT CRITERIA	SPECIFICATIONS
Scenario	My classroom
Driving Question	How do illustrations and text help people understand who I am?
Expectations	Write a paragraph and illustrate it with a picture of myself
Patron	Principal
Format	Note

FIGURE 3.21 Entry Event Criteria Reference

ENTRY EVENT CRITERIA	SPECIFICATIONS
Scenario	The specific context in which students address the driving question is presented during the entry event.
Driving Question	A key question that links the scenario or context to the key learning intention at the transfer level. The driving question may be presented directly during the presentation or embedded within the document as a statement requiring students to identify the question.
Expectations	Learning intentions and success criteria are often laid out in the entry event. Due dates are often found in the entry event. Culminating tasks required of students are presented from the outset of the project process.

(Continued)

FIGURE 3.21 (Continued)

ENTRY EVENT CRITERIA	SPECIFICATIONS
Patron	The individual or team of people who are seeking and expecting an answer to the driving question from the students. Though teachers are typically assessing student performance, often the project is presented to someone outside the classroom. These individuals should be clearly identified during the entry event process and on any documentation.
Format	Various methods can be used to convey the entry event information, including written instructions, multimedia presentations, and live presentations

FIGURE 3.22 Entry Event Criteria Example 2

ENTRY EVENT CRITERIA	SPECIFICATIONS
Scenario	Guinea worm outbreak
Driving Question	What strategies should we use to persuade community members to reflect on and perhaps change their behavior [specifically, as it relates to obesity]?
Expectations	Meet success criteria requirements. Students will • use motivational strategies to persuade an organization to change its procedures. • write out and orally present instructions for how to use motivational strategies to convince others. • demonstrate sensitivity to the particular context and cultural norms when offering their suggestions.
Task	Develop an action plan.
Audience	City council
Format	3-minute YouTube video and supplemental document outlining the recommended action plan and suggestions for motivational strategies

FIGURE 3.23 Project Example: Opinion Piece

PROJECT DESIGN

STEP 1: Learning Intention(s)

"I can write opinion piece(s) with details."

STEP 2: Success Criteria

Surface	Deep	Transfer
• I can list my opinions. • I can list other opinions.	• I can relate my opinions with those of others. • I can put those ideas into sentences.	• I can argue through writing my opinions and those of others.

STEP 3: Driving Question(s)

How do I write an opinion piece on something important to me?

Context

- Friends
- The environment
- Food
- Technology
- Sports

STEP 4: Tasks

Surface	Deep	Transfer
• Think-Pair-Share on exemplar opinion pieces. • Coconstruct a task checklist. • Brainstorm opinions on screen time. • Highlight opinions on screen time.	• Create a Venn diagram that shows like and dislike opinions. • Write opinions in paragraph form.	• Construct draft opinion document on screen time.

STEP 5: Entry Event

Scenario . . . Kindergarten class is asking about screen time.
Expectations . . . First graders craft an opinion piece.
Audience . . . Kindergarten
Format. . . . Written documentation

FIGURE 3.24 Entry Event Example

Dear First Graders,

As a kindergarten class, we are very interested to get your opinion on whether we should have the opportunity to use computers in our classroom. We have heard that watching the screen can hurt our eyes, prevent us from being social with one another, and prevent us from learning to our full potential! We know that you have used computers this year, and we would like to learn from your experience. Because we are working on reading and writing, our teachers thought it would be good to have you write your opinions down on paper and present them to us in a few weeks. We are very interested in hearing from you and hope that you can share your view and that of others, along with supporting details (so we can tell our parents and other adults what first graders think!). Thank you,

K Team

CONCLUSION

As Deborah Taba and Hilda Elkins (1966) stated, "Teaching in the dark is a questionable practice" (as cited in Tomlinson & McTighe, 2006, p. 72). This chapter argues that learning in the dark is also a questionable practice; and, through specific steps, a teacher may shine a light on expectations to assist teachers and students in clearly understanding what is expected at all levels of learning. This chapter articulated the steps in project design that are necessary to improve student and teacher clarity and, correspondingly, student achievement and confidence. Because projects and problems are initiated in the classroom to students at the transfer level, it is paramount that learners have the support necessary to meet surface and deep requirements to achieve transfer-level demands. This requires the following: students are able to separate context from learning intentions; learners have a clear understanding of surface to deep to transfer criteria; a driving question provides transfer-level opportunities; tasks are rich in reading, writing, and talking; and an entry event frames their learning. This level of clarity of expectations will enable students to better progress toward established goals and address a multitude of problems outside the one offered in the class by the teacher—which is the ultimate goal of transfer.

QUESTIONS FOR REFLECTION

- Do your current projects provide students with the clarity needed to separate the context of the problem and the underlying learning intentions? If so, what are they key aspects that ensure this happens? If not, what next steps will you take to provide this level of clarity?

- How do you currently ensure that students have an understanding of the need to have surface, deep, and transfer understanding or skill?

- How do you ensure that students are focused primarily on the learning intentions and success criteria and secondarily on the context?

- How do you provide choice in instructional tasks for students to demonstrate their understanding? How often do those instructional tasks require reading, writing, and talking?

- How will you develop an entry event that will prompt students to identify questions they need answered at surface, deep, and transfer expectations?

- How could you provide students with other problems in different contexts that enable them to transfer their learning?

ACTIVITIES

Activity 3.1 **Begin Designing a Project**

A complete project template is provided for you to begin designing a project. Complete all of the sections with the exception of the workshops and project calendar section. (This will be reviewed in the next chapter.) By completing this section, you will gain a deeper understanding of the key learning in this chapter and in the activities that follow.

PROJECT DESIGN		
STEP 1: Learning Intention(s)		
STEP 2: Success Criteria		
Surface	Deep	Transfer
STEP 3: Driving Question(s)		
Context		
STEP 4: Tasks		
Surface	Deep	Transfer

(Continued)

(Continued)

STEP 5: Entry Event
Scenario . . .
Expectations . . .
Patron . . .
Format . . .

Activity 3.2 **Designing "Look Fors"**

Review your current learning intentions, success criteria, and tasks in class right now through a student lens. Ask the students:

Question 1: What are the key learning intentions you are working toward right now to meet the driving question?

"Look fors": Students are able to separate the context from the learning intention.

Question 2: Where are you in your learning? What are you working toward?

"Look fors": Students separate the task from the intention. Students describe success criteria as a progression from surface to deep to transfer.

Question 3: How does this task represent your understanding? What other tasks have you taken on to meet expectations? What have you learned through those tasks?

"Look fors": Students separate the task from the intention. Students see there are multiple ways of demonstrating understanding.

Activity 3.3 **Evaluating Breadcrumbs in an Entry Event**

Find an entry event and attempt to identify the learning intentions and success criteria of the project. (Instructor) Ask yourself, *Where am I going* in this project? Are you able to determine the surface, deep, and transfer expectations? Can you separate the context from the actual learning intention? Who is the audience? What are the breadcrumbs that prime students to ask questions about success criteria? Do you find that the task is requiring reading, writing, and talking?

Next, identify the strengths, challenges, and next steps you would take to improve the entry event.

Activity 3.4   Building Breadcrumbs in an Entry Event

Practice building an entry event using the following letter template. Don't forget your breadcrumbs!

ENTRY EVENT TEMPLATE

Title

Dear _____,

- Scenario
- Driving Questions
- Expectations
- Task

Sincerely,

- Patron

Activity 3.5   Building a Task Matrix

The following matrix is a tool to support teachers in mapping out tasks that align with surface, deep, and transfer expectations and ensure that students have an appropriate amount of reading, writing, talking, and performing. As you go through designing your project (see Activity 3.1), pencil in activities that you may have students engage in to meet success criteria. A sample task matrix is provided following the task matrix template.

TASK MATRIX TEMPLATE

SUCCESS CRITERIA			
	Surface Requires a learner to understand single or multiple ideas or skills related to the core content or 21st century skills standards	**Deep** Requires a learner to relate single and multiple ideas or skills together to further understand core content or skills	**Transfer** Requires a learner to transfer his understanding and skills to situations outside of classroom context
TASK TYPE			
Reading Requires a learner to understand narrative and expository writing and convey meaning and inference			
Writing Requires a learner to convey understanding through a variety of written forms			
Talking Requires a learner to articulate understanding, give and receive feedback, and generate next steps with others			
Other			

 Available for download at **us.corwin.com/rigorouspblbydesign** under the "Preview" tab

Learning Intention: Students are able to describe the flow of information from transcription of ribonucleic acid (RNA) in the nucleus to translation of proteins on ribosomes.

SUCCESS CRITERIA			
	Surface *Requires a learner to understand single or multiple ideas or skills related to the core content or 21st century skills standards*	**Deep** *Requires a learner to relate single and multiple ideas or skills together to further understand core content or skills*	**Transfer** *Requires a learner to transfer her understanding and skills to situations outside of classroom context*
TASK TYPE			
Reading *Requires a learner to understand narrative and expository writing and convey meaning and inference*	• Students preview text-based resources to identify key terms.	• Students read primary sources on current work in the field of protein synthesis.	• Students read primary sources on current work in the field of protein synthesis, particular to context of project.
Writing *Requires a learner to convey understanding through a variety of written forms*	• Literature review (draft I)	• Students will develop an outline or graphic organizer detailing the differences between the structure and function of various organelles that are involved in protein synthesis. • Literature review (draft II)	• Students will submit a lab report indicating various factors that influence the protein synthesis process.

(Continued)

(Continued)

TASK TYPE			
Talking *Requires a learner to articulate understanding, give and receive feedback, and generate next steps with others*	• Students will discuss key ideas with partners and share in a larger group.	• Students will explain the key aspects of primary source documents in triads and relate those ideas to current understanding of proteins.	• Students will develop a matrix that details various drug combinations to address retrovirus manipulation of a cell's protein synthesis process. Student groups will present their matrices to a panel of experts and explain their solution choice. Students will be required to make predictions based on a series of questions and relate their predictions to key scientific principles.
Other			• Students will develop a slide deck to convey their understanding.

The following activity may be used by teachers to evaluate projects or for students to evaluate the efficacy of a project in meeting clarity expectations. Simply provide others with the project template or entry document and have them use the following chart to evaluate the project against clarity-based expectations.

CLARITY CHECKLIST

CLARITY	
Clear Learning Intentions	☐
• Students have a clear understanding of what they are expected to know and be able to do.	
Success Criteria	☐
• Students have a clear understanding of surface-, deep-, and transfer-level expectations to meet established learning outcomes throughout the project phases (Phase 1 through Phase 4).	
• Success criteria are void of project contexts and do not include task-specific requirements.	
Task Arrangement	☐
• Students have tasks that are aligned with surface-, deep-, and transfer-level expectations. Tasks are rich in reading, writing, and talking.	

In the following project, learners are provided with systematic details on an ailing patient at a nearby hospital. The health professionals at the hospital are interested to learn about the students' ability to discern the diagnosis, identify a potential treatment plan, and craft a prospective prognosis. The health professionals will be attending a special presentation in a few short weeks to understand how learners were able to use the science of cell biology, microbiology, and immunology to address the needs of the patient.

- What are the learning intentions of the project?

- What are the success criteria of the project at the surface, deep, and transfer levels?

- What other contexts could be used to meet the learning intentions and success criteria?

Sample Learning Intentions: We are learning to

- construct an explanation based on evidence for how the structure of DNA determines the structure of proteins that carry out the essential functions of life through systems of specialized cells (HS-LS1-1).

- construct and revise an explanation based on evidence for how carbon, hydrogen, and oxygen from sugar molecules may combine with other elements to form amino acids and/or other large carbon-based molecules (HS-LS1-6).

Sample Success Criteria

- Define *macromolecules*.

- Relate the structure and function of macromolecules.

- Apply our understanding of macromolecules to cellular disruption.

Other Considerations

- The challenge with this project is it is extremely context rich and could go in multiple directions. As this project could have multiple learning intentions and success criteria, the key is to establish clear learning outcomes and success criteria, and to identify what prior knowledge students possess. At certain grade levels, students may be ready to focus more on immunology and physiology rather than basic cell biology, and therefore the goals and requirements would shift.

Next Steps

- Construct a project using the aforementioned template,

- Provide the entry document to a student or teacher and have them identify the key learning intentions and success criteria.

- Based on the feedback received by teachers and students, revise the project to ensure alignment between learning intentions, success criteria, tasks, and the entry document.

Activity 3.8   Project Snapshot: Perspective and Understanding Assumptions (see also Figure 3.4)

In the following projects, learners are expected to write a persuasive essay on the critical importance of perspective and understanding assumptions to gain clarity and empathy for others and to understand the implications of how inferences, claims, and perspective, if left unchecked, can form actions that have unintended consequences. Learners engage in reading *Beowulf* and Grendel and excerpts from various pieces on the general Islamic population and current news reports to determine the power of perspective and its critical role in driving decision making at an individual, community, and international level.

- What are the learning intentions of the project?
- What are the success criteria of the project at the surface, deep, and transfer levels?
- What other contexts could be used to meet the learning intentions and success criteria?

Sample Learning Intention(s)

- to write a persuasive essay
- to understand how perspective and assumptions influence human behavior

SAMPLE SUCCESS CRITERIA

Learning Intention: to write a persuasive essay	Learning Intention: to understand how perspective and assumptions influence human behavior
Success criteria:	**Success criteria:**
Essay includes	To meet the learning intention I must
<ul><li>a thesis statement,</li><li>two or more quotes to back up the thesis statement,</li><li>two or more forms of data to back up the thesis statement,</li><li>two or more quotes and data to challenge the thesis statement, and</li><li>concluding paragraph that supports the thesis statement.</li></ul>	<ul><li>define bias, perspective, and assumption,</li><li>relate bias, perspective, and assumption in human interactions,</li><li>analyze strategies (such as questioning) that help people understand multiple perspectives and assumptions, and</li><li>apply the implications of bias, perspective, and assumption in a real-life situation that involves problem solving to promote greater clarity of multiple perspectives in decision making.</li></ul>

(Continued)

(Continued)

<table>
<tr><td>

Other Considerations

- If students have already mastered writing persuasive essays, you may want to provide various options for demonstrating their understanding and application of perspective and assumptions.

- During implementation, teachers may want to use different contexts and books for students to explore perspective and assumptions to influence human behavior. As students go through the project, they should have the opportunity to talk with students in different classes about their experiences and key learnings. Perhaps, students could use the success criteria and evaluate other class project tasks to gain a better understanding of the learning intentions and relate their own understanding of perspective and assumptions from one project context to another.

</td></tr>
<tr><td>

Next Steps

- Construct a project using the aforementioned template.

- Provide the entry document to a student or teacher and have them identify the key learning intentions and success criteria. Based on the feedback received by teachers and students, revise the project to ensure alignment between learning intentions, success criteria, tasks, and the entry document.

</td></tr>
</table>

NEXT STEPS

- Develop a project using the project design template in Appendix A.

- Develop a series of contexts for the project and have students vote for the one that is the most interesting.

- Begin with the end in mind by reflecting on a student's culminating presentation or product and identify how the student will represent surface, deep, and transfer expectations. Consider using Activity 3.5, Building a Task Matrix, to ensure balanced representation of surface, deep, and transfer expectations and that you have reading, writing, and talking tasks.

- Develop an entry event for the same project and ask a focus group of five or six students to identify the learning intentions and success criteria of the project. One way to engage the focus group in this process is to have them go through the Know/Need to Know Activity in the next chapter (see Activity 4.4).

- Consider seeking feedback using Protocol 5.1, Critical Friends Team (CFT).

CHAPTER 4

Design Shift II: Challenge
Structuring and Sequencing
Learning Through Projects

Students don't learn what we teach.

—Dylan Wiliam

In an interesting study, Derek Muller (2008) had students take a preassessment on physics concepts, watch videos (e.g., Khan Academy) to build knowledge on the standard, and then take a posttest. Muller found that students who watched videos felt like they had learned a great deal and felt confident in their understanding of the new material. However, after analyzing the results, Muller found that students performed at approximately the same level as they had during the pretest. Muller noticed that when students did not weigh their prior knowledge against new information and identify potential misconceptions, they reaffirmed past beliefs. In fact, Muller found that students

- thought they already knew the material,

- didn't pay utmost attention,

- didn't recognize that what was presented differed from what they were already thinking,

- didn't learn a thing, and

- became more confident in the ideas they had learned before.

Alternatively, when a second group of students were given the pretest and then shown a video that exposed common misconceptions of the learning intention, they increased their mental effort to understand the concept and, as a result, increased their learning. This exposure to a discrepancy between what the students thought they knew and the correct scientific information created a level of cognitive tension or a cognitive gap immediately motivated the students to resolve the disequilibrium that had been created. In other words, the students in the second group became curious when they realized that a cognitive gap existed and that there were ways to close the gap. This is why problems or projects should rely less on creating the elusive "engagement" that focuses on rich contexts that tie to student interest (though this should be considered) and move toward "perplexing" the mind by revealing the contradictions between prior knowledge and new knowledge. Additionally, teachers should direct their actions toward creating an awareness of these gaps and providing the support necessary to move student learning forward.

To meet this aim, the following two ideas are helpful to remember:

- **Align instruction, feedback, and learning strategies with levels of understanding (surface, deep, and transfer):** Teachers should understand what a student brings to the learning experience (i.e., prior knowledge) to plan instruction. As David Ausubel (1968, p. vi) stated, "The most important single factor influencing learning is what the learner already knows. Ascertain this and teach him accordingly." Students perform best when they are tasked with learning ideas and engaging in activities that are just outside their level of understanding. This is referred to as the Goldilocks (or just-right) principle. If the difficulty of the information to be learned is too great, the student will not learn much and will become uninterested. On the other hand, if the information is too easy, the student will not feel challenged and will become bored. In order to have the highest probability of impacting learners at the surface, deep, and transfer levels, the instruction strategies and feedback need to be specifically tailored to each individual student's particular level of understanding.

- **The process of identifying students' current progress and aligning teachers' actions is fluid and requires continual monitoring of learning and adjusting instruction:** To ensure that instruction, feedback, learning strategies, and activities are yielding the progress and proficiency desired, teachers and students must continually monitor student progress and proficiency and adjust their approach accordingly.

The previous chapter was focused on helping teachers support students in answering the question, *Where am I going?* This chapter focuses on the questions, *Where am I?* and *What's next?* In this chapter, teachers will hone their strategies for activating learning in their students by aligning teaching practices with the particular surface-, deep-, and transfer-level understanding of students. Once teachers ascertain the level of understanding, they can use the strategies presented here to plan ways to constantly assess student understanding and respond accordingly with tailored strategies that will have the greatest probability of advancing learning.

DESIGNING FOR CHALLENGE AND INTERVENTION

To create, recognize, and alleviate a student's cognitive gaps, teachers should consider the following two key steps:

Step 1 (Plan A): Align student activities and teaching actions according to surface, deep, and transfer expectations.

Step 2 (Plan B): Structure inquiry to identify student performance and provide support that aligns with the learning needs of students.

These steps may be best thought of as designing Plan A and Plan B for supporting students in their learning through a project. During Plan A, teachers spend time identifying the activities students will engage in during the project process (i.e., Phase 2 and Phase 3) at the appropriate level of challenge (surface, deep, and transfer). Moreover, teachers spend time thinking through how they will provide the right instructional strategies and feedback to support students through activities at the surface, deep, and transfer level. Teachers also think through the types of learning strategies they can offer students at surface-, deep-, and transfer-level success criteria to enable students to develop their confidence.

Plan B is the sequence of actions (i.e., tools and strategies) teachers take to handle the realities of implementation when Plan A doesn't fall exactly into place in the classroom. Invariably, a teacher's best laid plans will be augmented in light of learners' prior knowledge and performance during class. The realities of the classroom are that each student will bring a different level of prior knowledge and experience, and teachers need to be prepared to leverage that reality to make an impact on learning. Teachers need to continually understand students' understanding and identify the best interventions to support their learning. Plan B is, therefore, focused on routinizing inquiry into the daily lives of teachers and infusing inquiry into every routine with students.

STEP 1 (PLAN A): ALIGN STUDENT ACTIVITIES AND TEACHING ACTIONS ACCORDING TO SURFACE, DEEP, AND TRANSFER EXPECTATIONS

As discussed in previous chapters, clear expectations of learning are established upfront in problem-based learning (PBL) providing students with the surface-, deep-, and transfer-level expectations they need to understand to answer an overarching driving question on day one. Typically (depending on student prior knowledge) after the launch of the project, many students will likely need to engage in surface-level activities. Often surface-level strategies are more directive, emphasizing outlining, organizing, and previewing information while educators are providing direct instruction and giving direct feedback related to the task at hand. As students progress, different strategies are used to enable learners to think through relationships of concepts, ways to address problems, and means for thinking about their own thinking (i.e., metacognition). This section focuses on proactively aligning student and teacher actions that have a high probability of impacting students at surface, deep, and transfer levels.

There is a tremendous amount of research that suggests that the alignment or fit between a teacher's actions and a student's level of understanding is paramount to improving learning (Hattie & Donoghue, 2016; Hattie & Timperley, 2007; Marzano, 2007). For instance, Robert Marzano (2007) developed a framework for aligning instructional practices that support students who are encountering content for the first time (i.e., surface), practicing and deepening their understanding (i.e., deep), and engaging in cognitively complex tasks (i.e., transfer). The rationale is that based on students' cognitive gap between their existing understanding and the learning intention, specific strategies may enable learners to bridge the cognitive divide.

Similarly, John Hattie and Helen Timperley (2007) found that particular types of feedback have a higher effect at various stages of learning (surface, deep, and transfer). The thinking is that when learners are first encountering new information, they require task-specific feedback that enables them to understand if they are right or wrong. As they progress toward deeper learning, they require feedback that builds their awareness of potential errors (process) and how they can self-monitor (self-regulation). This trend appeared again in Hattie and Donoghue's (2016) review of research on learning strategies that students may use to enhance their own learning. Figure 4.1 shows an example of how instructional, feedback, and learning strategies align with surface, deep, and transfer levels.

Instructional, feedback, and learning strategies vary in effectiveness depending on whether the strategies are aligned with the student's needs relative to surface-, deep-, or transfer-level understanding.

In sum, instructional, feedback, and learning strategies vary in effectiveness depending on whether the strategies are aligned with the student's needs relative to surface-, deep-, or transfer-level understanding. Therefore, teachers should work to align instruction-, feedback-, and learning-based strategies with surface, deep, and transfer success criteria. Plan A focuses on

FIGURE 4.1 Aligning Teacher Actions With the Learning Needs of Students

LEARNING PROGRESSION	SURFACE	DEEP	TRANSFER
	Understanding one concept, idea, and/or skill	Understanding how concepts, ideas, and skills relate	Understanding how to transfer concepts and relationships between concepts to various contexts
INSTRUCTIONAL STRATEGIES	*Effective teaching strategies to enable students to develop understanding of core knowledge or skill*		
	• Previewing new content (KWL, advanced organizer)	• Examining similarities and differences (e.g., The teacher engages students in comparing, classifying, creating analogies and metaphors.)	• Engaging students in cognitively complex tasks (e.g., The teacher engages students in decision-making tasks, problem-solving tasks, investigative tasks.)
	• Chucking content into "digestible bites" (e.g., The teacher presents content in smaller portions.)		
	• Elaborating on new information (e.g., The teacher asks questions that require students to make and defend inferences.)	• Examining errors in reasoning (e.g., The teacher asks students to examine fallacies, propaganda, and bias.)	• Providing resources and guidance (e.g., The teacher makes resources available.)
	• Recording and representing knowledge		

(Continued)

FIGURE 4.1 (Continued)

LEARNING PROGRESSION		SURFACE	DEEP	TRANSFER
FEEDBACK STRATEGIES	*Effective forms of feedback to enable students to move forward in their learning*	Provide information to students that helps them think through the task at hand by • distinguishing correct from incorrect answers. • acquiring more or different information. • building more surface knowledge.	Provide information to students that helps them process • relationships between ideas. • finding ways to detect errors in thinking and engaging in activities.	Provide information to students that helps them self-regulate their learning by • creating ways to self-assess performance. • strategies to seek support in learning. • monitoring and investing in seeking and acting on feedback to improve.
LEARNING STRATEGIES	*Effective strategies students may use to assist them in their own learning*	• outlining • mnemonics • summarization • underlining and highlighting • note taking • deliberate practice • rehearsal	• seeking help from peers • classroom discussions • evaluation and reflection • self-verbalization and self-questioning • metacognitive strategies	• identifying similarities and differences in problems • seeing patterns in new situations

developing and sequencing lessons throughout the project. It is important to note here that lessons are referred to as *workshops* in the PBL environment. Plan A is accomplished through two substeps:

> Substep 1: Structuring workshops to align with surface, deep, and transfer success criteria

> Substep 2: Sequencing workshops to follow the surface, deep, and transfer progression

Substep 1: Structuring Workshops to Align With Surface, Deep, and Transfer Success Criteria

Workshops resemble a lesson and follow a typical lesson sequence for supporting student content development (see Figure 4.2). Workshops are developed to meet surface, deep, and transfer success criteria. Figure 4.3 provides an example of how a teacher may plan content-based workshops at the surface, deep, and transfer level.

FIGURE 4.2 Scope and Sequence of a Typical Workshop

1. **Review Know and Need to Know:** Students are invited or required to attend a workshop based on preassessment data (i.e., test, student request). Teachers work with students to recognize their current knowledge on the topic or application of a skill and then discuss discrepancies between their current understanding and expectations.

2. **Connection:** Students reflect on the overall purpose of their current work to the larger outcomes and project questions that they are working toward.

3. **Provide instructional strategy:** Teachers use instructional strategies based on student knowledge and skill. Students may discuss a learning strategy that has been impactful.

4. **Provide opportunities for practice:** Opportunities for practice (guided and independent) are provided and peers act as critical friends and resources to support the learning of all students. Teachers typically provide feedback to assist students in perfecting their practice and meeting success criteria.

5. **Review Need to Know:** Teachers and students typically review current understanding and progress, revise, or clarify past performance, current performance, and next steps. They clarify what they understand or know and what they are still working toward understanding or need to know.

6. **Inspect student outcomes:** Teachers provide opportunities for evaluating and reflecting on performance. Teachers and students check back with individuals and teams to make sure growth and proficiency is occurring.

FIGURE 4.3 Workshop Examples at Surface, Deep, and Transfer Levels

PROJECT DESIGN		
STEP 1: Learning Intention(s)		
The industrialized nations' desire for abundant resources and new markets for their goods coupled with feelings of cultural superiority (such as Social Darwinism), and increased military power allowed for and encouraged imperial expansion. Imperialism had lasting positive and negative effects.		
STEP 2: Success Criteria		
Surface	Deep	Transfer
• Understands political, economic, or social influences of a nation on other nations	• Relates political, economic, and social influences of one nation on another	• Applies political economic, and social influences of nations on other nations as related to contemporary issues

Note: See Project 3 in Appendix B for a detailed layout of the project.

PROGRESSION	REQUIRED STUDENT TASK	INSTRUCTIONAL STRATEGIES	NEED TO KNOW STEMS . . .
Surface	Create an outline.	• demonstrations, brief practice test, or exercise questioning	What are the reasons for nations to occupy other nations?
Deep	Create a Venn diagram.	• nonlinguistic representation • summarizing • identifying similarities and differences (comparing, contrasting, classifying)	Which nations of the world were considered powerful in the late 1800s, and why they were considered so? What impact did the powerful nations have on the political, economic, and social development of nations considered less powerful?

PROGRESSION	REQUIRED STUDENT TASK	INSTRUCTIONAL STRATEGIES	NEED TO KNOW STEMS . . .
Transfer	Write a paper extending comparisons between problems.	• generating and testing hypotheses, extended comparison (creating metaphors, creating analogies)	In what ways have recent conflicts between some Middle Eastern nations and the United States and Great Britain reflected previous historical patterns? How have previous patterns been disrupted to promote better relations between countries?

To create a workshop that has a high probability of making an impact on student learning, the following questions should be considered by teachers:

- **Surface Level:** What instructional approaches will support students in understanding foundational knowledge (e.g., facts, vocabulary terms) related to learning outcomes? What types of feedback will support students in understanding single and multiple ideas and the task at hand? What learning strategies will enable students to better engage with surface-level success criteria?

- **Deep Level:** What instructional approaches support students in connecting and contrasting ideas? What are generalizations and principles that can be made about these ideas? What types of feedback will support students in understanding single and multiple ideas and the task at hand? What learning strategies will enable students to better engage with surface-level success criteria?

- **Transfer Level:** What instructional approaches support students in applying the learning outcomes to project expectations? What types of feedback will support students in understanding single and multiple ideas and the task at hand? What learning strategies will enable students to better engage with surface-level success criteria?

Figure 4.4 (transfer), Figure 4.5 (deep), and Figure 4.6 (surface) provide a few suggested instructional strategies that have a high probability of impacting student learning at the appropriate level of learning. These instructional strategies have been selected because they directly model effective learning strategies at the surface, deep, and transfer level. The following strategies are but a few of a multitude of instructional strategies in existence; they can be embedded within workshops and included on your project template.

FIGURE 4.4 Suggested *Transfer-Learning* Instructional Strategies

INSTRUCTIONAL STRATEGY	DESCRIPTION	"NEED TO KNOW"
Providing support for claims and findings errors	Teachers task students with finding claims that support and refute arguments. In addition, students are analyzing similar patterns.	What evidence do we have to substantiate our claims? What evidence is available to substantiate counterclaims? How do experts in the field perceive the problem? How do these perceptions differ from others?
Extended comparison (creating metaphors, creating analogies)	Students draw direct comparisons between two issues to clarify similarities and differences.	What are ways to interpret the issue or problem? How are those interpretations similar and different to other problems, situations, and disciplines?
Generating and testing hypotheses	Students are tasked with identifying answers to problems and then using resources to identify whether those answers are legitimate.	What are possible answers to the question or problem we are facing? How can we test our assumptions?
Comparing and contrasting problems	Students investigate similarities and differences between types of problems.	What are the similarities and differences between these problems? How does this relate to this academic discipline? How would this apply elsewhere?

FIGURE 4.5 Suggested *Deeper-Learning* Instructional Strategies

INSTRUCTIONAL STRATEGY	DESCRIPTION	"NEED TO KNOW"
Examining similarities and differences	Teachers engage students in comparing, classifying, creating analogies, and metaphors. Students may be tasked with creating representations of similarities and differences (comparing, contrasting, and classifying) through nonlinguistic representations (e.g., graphic organizer).	How do certain ideas relate and connect?

INSTRUCTIONAL STRATEGY	DESCRIPTION	"NEED TO KNOW"
Examining errors in reasoning	Teachers provide various representations of how ideas relate. Students generate a representation of new information that does not rely on language.	How do certain perspectives influence our understanding of concepts and principles and their application?

FIGURE 4.6 Suggested *Surface-Learning* Instructional Strategies

INSTRUCTIONAL STRATEGY	DESCRIPTION	"NEED TO KNOW"
Elaborative interrogation	A strategy for generating an explanation for why a stated fact is true Students should begin this process by identifying what they know about the fact or idea. Next, they may preview content on the Web or in text-based resources. From here, the students may engage in a discussion of their prior knowledge and what they have found from resources to determine why a statement is true.	"Why is this true?" "Why does it make sense that . . . ?" "Why would this fact be true for [X] but not for [Y]?"
Jigsaw	A cooperative strategy where a topic is divided into sections, and each student (or group of students) is responsible for previewing, outlining, and presenting an idea Each student or student group shares the topic with other students and addresses questions that they may have.	"What are the key ideas of this topic?" "Why are these ideas important?"

(Continued)

FIGURE 4.6   (Continued)

INSTRUCTIONAL STRATEGY	DESCRIPTION	"NEED TO KNOW"
Perspective analysis	A strategy for questioning and exploring an idea from multiple vantage points. The strategy typically follows a five-step process: 1. Identify a position on a controversial topic. 2. Determine the reasoning behind the position. 3. Identify an opposing or several opposing positions. 4. Describe the reasoning behind the positions. 5. Summarize key learning.	1. "What do I believe about this? What are key beliefs about this topic?" 2. "Why do I or others believe this?" 3. "What are other ways of looking at this?" 4. "Why might someone else hold a different opinion?" 5. "What have I learned?"

Substep 2: Sequence Workshops to Follow the Surface, Deep, and Transfer Progression

This book anchors workshops in a progression of learning by first previewing transfer expectations and then structuring surface- to deep- to transfer-level learning through workshops. Workshops follow a sequence from introducing the problem and then building competency over the time of the project to eventually have enough understanding to effectively solve the driving question.

One way to do this is to place workshops on a project calendar in the following way: transfer to surface to deep to transfer. As a designer is mapping this work on a calendar, he or she should consider how these workshops support students in answering the driving question. The suggestion here is to cluster the workshops in a way that adheres to a straightforward problem-solving process. This text uses the following three steps (an abbreviated form of the problem-solving process articulated in Thomas Harvey, William Bearley, and Sharon Corkrum's [1997] *The Practical Decision Maker: A Handbook for Decision Making and Problem Solving in Organizations*):

1. **Building Understanding of the Problem and Expectations for a Solution:** During Phases 1, 2, and 3 of the project, students are identifying and clarifying the driving question, tasks, and expectations of the project. Students are introduced to the project and begin developing surface- and deeper-level knowledge and skills. The content and

skill knowledge form the basis to the solution of the driving question. Teachers are often providing feedback at the task level (see Figure 4.1).

2. **Transferring Understanding and Creating Solutions:** During Phase 3, students develop deeper knowledge and skill and are clear on project expectations. As such, students begin investigating potential solutions and eventually selecting a solution that is amiable to the patron and to each other. When generating solutions, "the more the merrier! In the complex world of rapid change good solutions are often derived by combining parts of a number of ideas and by building on them." (Harvey, Bearley, & Corkrum, p. 27). Solution generation is a divergent process requiring substantial inquiry-based skills. Solution selection on the other hand, is a convergent process requiring clear decision-making agreements. Students are now ready for Phase 4. Teachers are often providing feedback at the process level.

3. **Implementing and Inspecting Solutions:** During Phase 4, students carefully plan, act, and review their solutions or answers to the driving question. In the project environment, this may be a presentation or the second or third draft of a paper. Teachers are often providing feedback at the self-regulation level.

Project calendars are structured to sequence the aforementioned three problem-solving steps and surface-, deep-, and transfer-level workshops across an estimated time of meeting transfer-level expectations. Figure 4.7 illustrates a generic project calendar template and Figure 4.8 provides an example of a project calendar.

FIGURE 4.7 Project Calendar Model

PROJECT CALENDAR					
	Monday	Tuesday	Wednesday	Thursday	Friday
Week 1 [Phase 1 and Phase 2]	Launch project	Surface and deep workshops	Surface and deep workshops	Surface and deep workshops	Assessment workshops
Week 2 [Phase 2 and Phase 3]	Surface and deep workshops	Transfer workshop	Assessment solution generation	Transfer workshop	Solution selection workshops
Week 3 [Phase 3 and Phase 4]	Workshops and preparation	Draft presentation feedback	Workshops and preparation	Presentation	Debriefing

 Available for download at **us.corwin.com/rigorouspblbydesign** under " the "Preview" tab

FIGURE 4.8 Project Calendar Example

PROJECT CALENDAR					
	Monday	Tuesday	Wednesday	Thursday	Friday
Week 1 [Phase 1 and Phase 2]	Project launch Preassessment	Surface workshop(s) (Define terms)	Surface workshop(s) (Sources and conditions)	Pair discussions/ Jigsaw (Sources and conditions)	Pair discussions/ Jigsaw (Sources and conditions)
Week 2 [Phase 2 and Phase 3]	Deep workshops(s) Ideological conflict Case study review Provide graphic organizer draft.	Deep workshop(s) Conflict snapshot Case study review Construct graphic organizer.	Deep workshop(s) Conflict snapshot Case study review Feedback on graphic organizer	Deep workshop(s) Review US actions. Complete graphic organizer.	Deep workshop(s) Review white paper exemplars.
Week 3 [Phase 3 and Phase 4]	Transfer workshops Current issues Current solutions Assessment Brainstorm	Transfer workshops Current issues (looking at different contexts) Develop white paper.	Transfer workshops Critical friends on white paper Prepare 5-minute presentation.	Present solution. Submit paper. Discuss new topics.	Reflect

Note: To read the full Imperialism project, see Project 3: Changing or Maintaining Our Imperialist Imperative in Appendix B.

 Available for download at **us.corwin.com/rigorouspblbydesign** under "The "Preview" Tab

Figure 4.9 illustrates an expanded template that integrates the steps of Design Shift I (clarity) and the scope and sequence of workshops necessary to build surface-, deep-, and transfer-learning outcomes. The next section of the chapter focuses on Plan B and how to use assessment practices and inquiry to identify student understanding and respond accordingly.

FIGURE 4.9 Expanded Template

PROJECT DESIGN		
STEP 1: Learning Intention(s)		
STEP 2: Success Criteria		
Surface	Deep	Transfer
STEP 3: Driving Question(s)		
Context		
STEP 4: Tasks		
Surface	Deep	Transfer
STEP 5: Entry Event		
Scenario . . .		
Expectations . . .		
Patron . . .		
Format . . .		
WORKSHOPS		
Surface	Deep	Transfer

PROJECT CALENDAR					
	Monday	Tuesday	Wednesday	Thursday	Friday
Week 1 *[Phase 1 and Phase 2]*					
Week 2 *[Phase 2 and Phase 3]*					
Week 3 *[Phase 3 and Phase 4]*					

Note: For a detailed example of an elementary science project, see Project 1 in Appendix B.

Maren Rocca-Hunt
Executive Director, Elementary Education
Napa Valley Unified School District
Napa, CA
www.nvusd.k12.ca.us

I began working as a principal for Napa Valley Unified School District (NVUSD) twelve years ago. Project-based learning was, and remains, the central pedagogy for New Tech High School. The NVUSD Board of Trustees recognized the need to expand student learning to include the 4Cs (collaboration, critical thinking, communication, and creativity) as a response to their view of student achievement. After many years of NCLB [No Child Left Behind], the singular focus on foundational skills appeared to have stalled for most students and specifically for our neediest learners. The current superintendent was hired specifically to address our need to address English learners/Latino students as our demographics began to shift, as well as to expand opportunities for all students to benefit from PBL beyond one small high school. However, we have broadened the vision beyond PBL and now use Inquiry-based learning. This shift looks at different approaches such as International Baccalaureate, Arts Integration, and Dual Immersion in addition to PBL based on either the BIE [Buck Institute of Education] or New Tech Network models.

Hindsight is always 20/20, and many districts struggle to fully implement well. As a district, we struggled with implementation, by which I mean building adult knowledge, understanding, and skill that results in changes in classroom instruction, strategies such as direct instruction, reciprocal teaching, data teams, and professional learning communities. As a system, some schools opted in, others declined. We had some growth in results such as CAASPP [California Assessment of Student Performance and Progress], graduation rates, and A–G [high school course subject and academic rigor requirements for University of California admissions]. Although the gap is closing, there still exists a gap for English language learners, Latinos, and African Americans. We also did not expand our understanding of or response to the needs of English learners. We learned over the past few years how difficult it is to build instructional knowledge and expertise in literacy and math at the same time we asked teachers to shift to a PBL/inquiry-based approach. So we created the pendulum and struggled with the foundational skills versus PBL camps. Full-scale implementation must be carefully planned and inclusive, and it must address the inclusion of both foundational skill development and PBL/inquiry-based learning experiences. It must also allow for adult learning while focusing on results for students. It is not easy, but it is worth the challenge.

Over time, my perspective has become more balanced and accepting, where individuals are in their professional development in both instructional design and the use of data to inform that practice. Throughout the last few years, I have seen both sides of the argument, and I see the need and urgency to address expanding and understanding and application of student data in both Inquiry-based instruction and high-impact instruction.

We have created (using Fullan's New Pedagogies for Deeper Learning) systems to bring schools together across the district to collaborate on inquiry-based units of instruction. This has pushed the ability of the system to address the impact of instruction for students more fully and involve all participants regardless of their pedagogical focus (IB, PBL, NTN, Artful Learning, etc.). We have also expanded to the 6 Cs, adding character and citizenship to our work and focusing on how to measure impact on student learning.

In hindsight, had I to do it over again, I might have started off by building a culture at all levels of the organization including the district office. System change is difficult and requires learning throughout; we could have been more purposeful as learners.

As we move forward, my colleagues and I are trying to avoid decisions or trainings that exclude either "side" of the work. If we have trainings or learning about instruction, we make sure it addresses or asks questions about inquiry as well as focuses on skill- and content-building strategies. We want to make our work about both PBL/inquiry-based and foundational skill instruction and have results demonstrating all students are learning and growing. Our goal is to close the learning gap so that all students are excelling.

STEP 2 (PLAN B): STRUCTURE INQUIRY TO IDENTIFY STUDENT PERFORMANCE AND PROVIDE SUPPORT THAT ALIGNS WITH THE LEARNING NEEDS OF STUDENTS

Inquiry as Intervention: Four Questions to Include as Part of Any Routine

- Where am I going in my learning?

- Where am I now in my learning?

- What next steps am I going to take in my learning?

- How do I improve my learning and that of others?

One way to plan for Plan B is to ensure that inquiry is infused in day-to-day routines as a means of intervention. As discussed earlier, we know that learning is largely predicated on a student's prior knowledge and experiences and every student's prior knowledge and experience is different. Therefore, in any given routine, what a student is experiencing will be interpreted differently, and every, student's understanding will vary. As Graham Nuthall (2005) states,

> Knowing that a student is busily engaged in an activity does not tell you what (or how) the student is learning. You need to know exactly what information or knowledge is engaging the student's mind. To give a simplified example, it is not enough to say that a student learned because the student was busy reading a book unless you also identify what the student was reading and how that content related to what the student already knew . . . . What has not changed is the mythical belief that engaging in learning activities (such as listening to a teacher talking, discussing the results of an experiment, or writing a report of an investigation) transfers the content of the activity to the mind of the student. (pp. 917–922)

> To make a real impact on kids, educators must find out what each student is thinking during any activity and, from that evidence, make decisions on what steps are needed to enhance their learning.

This is why Dylan Wiliam's (2011) quote, "Students do not learn what we teach" (p. 47) is so powerful. There is no direct correlation between a routine, an activity, or a presentation and what is acquired in the mind of a learner. Corresponding, educators often make very powerful and erroneous assumptions about student learning based on what the students are doing in an activity and the beliefs teachers have about a student. To make a real impact on kids, educators must find out what each student is thinking during any activity and, from that evidence, make decisions on what steps are needed to enhance their learning. This is why "learning by doing" is a dangerous adage because it misses the "checking and conversation" elements that are so critical. Yes, people learn by doing but what they learn varies and that variance must be understood and leveraged rather than assumed. We must test assumptions and the recommended means of doing that is through inquiry. Inquiry allows teachers to constantly assess where students are in their learning and, from that understanding, engage with appropriate interventions. As Larissa McLean Davies and colleagues (2013) state,

> Assess the learning and learning needs of every student and provide appropriate interventions to move that learning forward. Teachers must also have the professional capabilities to evaluate the impact they are having on each student. . . . [T]eachers must be expert in gathering evidence and using sound clinical judgment to create appropriate learning strategies to meet each learner's needs. Clinical judgment is only possible when the practice is underpinned by a well-defined body of knowledge, keen observational

skills and highly developed analytical skills. . . . Assessment of student work as evidence learning lies at the core . . . , a key underlying principle being that with a data-driven, evidence-based approach to teaching and learning, teachers can manipulate the learning environment and scaffold learning for every student, regardless of the student's development or intellectual capacity. (pp. 96–98)

Often in PBL, interventions from teachers occur, but they are focused on student progress toward completing a project task, meeting deadlines, and satisfying group-dynamics problems and are not always centered at the heart of student learning: interpreting new information and assimilating or challenging previous beliefs. John Mergendoller and John Thomas (2005) found that some teachers used frequent, short progress conferences to identify progress toward set benchmarks, articulate due dates, and support student-led discussions. Progress conferences as a routine may or may not have an impact depending on the level of focus on learning and the level of intervention in light of evidence of learning progress and proficiency. Information regarding student prior knowledge, misunderstandings, and growth in learning and intervention is dependent on the actions of teachers. This is where progress conferences have the most leverage. Such progress conferences may be leveraged with a series of structured questions within a teacher's established routines, enabling teachers, students, and peers to focus on, talk about, and take action on learning.

Formative Teaching as Routine

During the process of students moving from surface to deep learning, their prior knowledge needs to be exposed, tested, and changed. The recommendation here is that teachers in the PBL classroom use four essential questions to drive learning from surface to deep to transfer. These four questions are largely based on the Assessment for Learning (AfL) research. *AfL* or *formative assessment* practice may be defined as *the use of achievement evidence to adapt what happens in the classroom to meet learner needs.* James Popham (2013) refers to formative assessment as an ends-means process, meaning (1) students and teachers clearly understand the overall outcome or expectations (ends), (2) students and teachers understand current performance, and (3) students and teachers take action to enhance student learning. Formative assessment is an *active* process for both teachers and students to alleviate the gap by using the best available strategy. Formative teaching has the potential to yield a substantial impact on student learning because the practice clarifies learning outcomes to students (effect size 0.75), provides challenging yet manageable goals (effect size 0.56), offers and uses targeted feedback (effect size 0.73), provides multiple opportunities to learn the goals (i.e., mastery learning; effect size 0.58), and

> During the process of students moving from surface to deep learning, their prior knowledge needs to be exposed, tested, and changed.

aligns instructional and learning strategies that target surface-, deep-, and transfer-level learning. Even more, student motivation is enhanced when the clarity of the knowledge (ends) gap has been identified and the way (means) to address the gap has been established.

The simple message is to "Mind the Gap" (i.e., throughout the project, from beginning to end, enable students to address the cognitive dissonance they are experiencing at the moment). The means to address the gap is for teachers to continually find the answers to the following four questions from students:

- Where am I going in my learning?

- Where am I now in my learning?

- What next steps am I going to take in my learning?

- How do I improve my learning and that of others?

Question 1: Where am I going in my learning?

Question 1 addresses a student's understanding of project expectations and underlying learning outcomes. Teachers must identify practices that they can utilize throughout the project that support students, individually and collectively, in understanding and articulating the learning outcomes of the project (see Figure 4.10).

Question 2: Where am I now in my learning?

Question 2 asks for a student's or teacher's current understanding and performance in light of the project expectations and underlying learning outcomes (see Figure 4.11). This requires two actions from students:

1. Students identify their level of understanding or skill relative to project expectations.

2. Students create a meaningful set of short-term goals and plans to meet learning outcomes and overall project expectations. These actions can be enhanced by peer and teacher assistance.

Question 3: What next steps am I going to take in my learning?

Question 3 requires teachers and students to offer and provide feedback to one another and then make decisions to enhance overall learning. Figure 4.12 offers strategies promote identification of next steps (*What next steps am I going to take in my learning?*).

Question 4: How do I improve my learning and that of others?

Question 4 is linked to two key purposes. First, the question promotes self-regulation and overall metacognition (see transfer learning strategies in Figure 4.1). Second, the question focuses on how learners support one another in their learning. The process of supporting collective learning will be discussed extensively in the next chapter. Figure 4.13 provides strategies to promote identification of self- and social improvement (*How do I improve my learning and that of others?*).

FIGURE 4.10 Strategies to Promote Clarity of Expectations
(*Where am I going in my learning?*)

DESCRIPTION	STRATEGY
Develop and review the driving question	Students review the entry event and identify the embedded driving question. Next, they separate the context from the key learning intention and success criteria. Students then post their responses in a manner that all other students and teachers can observe. From here, the teacher asks the class to devise a shared statement of the learning intention and success criteria.
Know and need to know list	Students draft two lists that identify what they understand (know) and what they lack in understanding (need to know).
Tune in and link	Teachers ask students to create a T-chart on a piece of paper and list the success criteria that are clear to them on one side of the paper and what is unclear on the other side of the piece of paper. Students share their papers in groups of three and develop a master list of the topics that are unclear. Teachers walk around "tuning" in (listening in on what is clear or confusing for students). Next, teachers share the common misunderstandings or "link" shared areas of confusion. Finally, the teacher discusses with students how they could better address areas of clarity by asking: *What could I/we do to provide clarity here? What could I/we do next time? What seemed to work for those areas that were crystal clear?*
Co-construct success criteria	Provide students with the learning intention of a project, and ask them to identify potential criteria for success. Next, capture all of the data and then have students review exemplar work and evaluate that work relative to the success criteria they developed. Ask students, what if any success criteria should be changed or added and why.

(Continued)

FIGURE 4.10 (Continued)

DESCRIPTION	STRATEGY
What am I bringing with me?	Beyond the Know/Need to Know list, teachers may want to offer a few different preassessments of where students are in their learning. This doesn't have to be a test but rather a short 5- to 10-minute activity that answers the question of "What am I bringing with me as I'm learning through this project?" Begin by giving each student 3 to 5 minutes to write down a response to the question. Next, give students a brief question or task to solve, such as • provide an error to a typical content question and ask, What do you notice about this problem and the solution? • give a solution to a problem and have students argue why that solution is correct (or not). • provide a solution and ask students to identify the number of ways they can solve the problem.

FIGURE 4.11 Strategies to Promote Clarity of Current Progress
(*Where am I now in my learning?*)

STRATEGY	DESCRIPTION
No hands up	A norm or agreement is established in the classroom where students are not expected or encouraged to raise their hand if they know an answer to a question posed by a teacher or a peer. Instead, teachers should ask students randomly to respond to questions associated with core content and student understanding of their own performance relative to established learning intentions and success criteria. By doing this, teachers gain a better sense of individual and collective understanding or knowledge gap. Students should have the opportunity to raise their hands if they have questions about key learning and their own progress. As such, if several hands go up, the teacher would have a better understanding of student understanding of their own competency and/or progress toward learning intentions and success criteria.

Playing Hoosier basketball	This strategy requires teachers to ask a question to the class and have at least five students provide a response. In other words, once a response from a student is made, the teacher "passes" the response to at least five other students before the teacher provides any response.
Letter cards	Students are provided with four index cards labeled *A, B, C*, and *D*. When asked a multiple-choice question by a teacher or student, students display their answer by lifting up one of the cards. They then confer with their small group to discuss their answers and make changes in light of peer review and feedback.
Daily review of key outcomes	Students take time to review key success criteria and task criteria to identify where they are in their learning, set short-term goals, and take action to meet those goals. Once developed, they discuss their goals and current progress with other students and then submit an exit ticket to teachers to review their responses.

FIGURE 4.12 Strategies to Promote Clarity of Next Steps
(*What next steps am I going to take in my learning?*)

STRATEGY	DESCRIPTION
Comments-only assessment	Teachers or students provide feedback to others only via comments and provide no metric-level assessment that could be used to compare students to others. Comments are related to learning intentions and success criteria.
Give students work to move forward (strips).	Teachers provide a group of students their assessed work and a series of comments that are on separate strips of paper. The strips of paper with comments are separate from the assessed work, and the group has to figure out what comments go with what paper.
Two-thirds assessment	Typical summative assessments (e.g., tests) are conducted two-thirds of the way through the project to ensure that students and teachers have enough time to take corrective action and to explore other means to represent understanding.

FIGURE 4.13 Strategies to Promote Clarity of Self- and Social Improvement
(*How do I improve my learning and that of others?*)

STRATEGY	DESCRIPTION
Identify key strategies to meet outcomes.	Learners reflect on key learning strategies that they have used. Next, they identify the efficacy of those strategies by evaluating their progress toward meeting specific outcomes. They share their reflections with peers and then decide on a strategy they will use to achieve new learning outcomes.
Goal setting and planning	Learners take a preassessment to inform their learning goals. Learners then craft next steps to meet stated goals, share those goals with peers, and receive feedback on their goals and action steps to inform their final plan for meeting personal goals.
Critical friends process	Learners sit in a circle. One learner shares his or her performance data. Other learners ask clarifying questions to ensure they understand the information. Next, the presenter listens while the other learners share their thoughts on strengths, questions, and potential next steps.
Assessment tracker inspection	Students monitor their own learning on Google sheets by writing out their learning outcomes and marking progress on success criteria.
Randomize peers for discussions.	Switch students each week to collaborate about learning intentions and success criteria, and to give and receive feedback.

CONCLUSION

In project-based learning, teachers craft a series of workshops at the surface, deep, and transfer levels to provide the right level of challenge to develop students' level of competency. A key aspect of this work is identifying interventions or strategies (instruction, learning, and feedback) that fit with the three learning levels. Teachers then sequence surface to deep to transfer workshops on a calendar that aligns with a problem-solving process. Teachers also prepare for continually assessing student learning through a series of inquiry-based strategies that visualizes student understanding. Through this process, teachers can provide the necessary intervention to move student learning forward from surface, to deep, to transfer. This process also enables students to begin reflecting on their own learning, how to improve their learning, and how to take part in and invite others in the process of learning as a community.

QUESTIONS FOR REFLECTION

- What are ways that you can identify students' prior knowledge? How do you use that knowledge to identify next steps for a student, group of students, and the class? How do you support students in understanding the discrepancies between what they know and need to know?

- What evidence do you gather to identify student progress?

- How do you structure the conversation to enable students to understand the "gap"? How do the four questions support these efforts? How does the Know/Need to Know list support you in this work?

- What are instructional strategies that you use in your discipline or in general that support students at the surface, deep, and transfer level?

- There is an adage in research that students "learn by doing." How will you ensure that students are learning what is expected during the doing process?

- What are ways that you can build capacity for students to engage in minding their own cognitive gap and using the four questions to drive their own learning and that of their peers?

- Reflecting on your current practice, how capable are your students in conveying their understanding prior to a lesson and their understanding after the lesson?

- How much of your conversations with students is on resource allocation or management, length of an activity, group structures, consequences or incentives based on completion of tasks relative to deadlines? How much time are students focusing their conversations on these factors?

ACTIVITIES

Activity 4.1   Building Workshops: "Filling Buckets"

Build a surface, deep, and transfer workshop using the following workshop elements. See Figure 4.3 for an example. Figures 4.4, 4.5, and 4.6 provide examples of transfer-, deep-, and surface-level instructional strategies accordingly.

SURFACE-LEVEL WORKSHOP ELEMENTS

SURFACE

- Review Know/Need to Know
- Connection
- Instructional Strategy
- Guided/Independent Practice
- Deliverables
- Review Need to Know
- Inspect Student Outcomes/Reinforce Practice

DEEP-LEVEL WORKSHOP ELEMENTS

DEEP

- Review Know/Need to Know
- Connection
- Instructional Strategy
- Guided/Independent Practice
- Deliverables
- Review Need to Know
- Inspect Student Outcomes/Reinforce Practice

TRANSFER-LEVEL WORKSHOP ELEMENTS

TRANSFER

- Review Know/Need to Know
- Connection
- Instructional Strategy
- Guided/Independent Practice
- Deliverables
- Review Need to Know
- Inspect Student Outcomes/Reinforce Practice

Calendars should always be in rough-draft form and revised continually. Consider taking 10 to 15 minutes to draft your calendar and be ready with pencil in hand to make changes. Here are a few steps to consider when building your calendar:

1. Use a pencil or .doc format.

2. Organize workshops across the surface-, deep-, and transfer-learning levels.

3. Sequence each phase to week allotments.

4. Establish benchmarks to check in on progress.

PROJECT CALENDAR TEMPLATE

PROJECT CALENDAR					
	Monday	Tuesday	Wednesday	Thursday	Friday
Week 1 [Phase 1 and Phase 2]					
Week 2 [Phase 2 and Phase 3]					
Week 3 [Phase 3 and Phase 4]					

Available for download at **us.corwin.com/rigorouspblbydesign** under the "Preview" tab

Begin using the four structured questions in your daily practice:

- Where am I going in my learning?

- Where am I now in my learning?

- What next steps am I going to take in my learning?

- How do I improve my learning and that of others?

As you begin using these questions, evaluate the amount of time you and your students are using inquiry to discuss management-oriented questions (i.e., related to project management, resources, group structures, tasks, grading, and rules) and learning-oriented questions (i.e., learning intentions, success criteria, prior knowledge, and learning strategies). One way to do this is to create a simple T-chart and jot down student and teacher responses to the four questions posed. An example of questions that may be asked are shown in the chart on the facing page. It may be helpful to have other teachers come in or students assist in analyzing management- and learning-oriented related questions.

INQUIRY ROUTINES T-CHART

INQUIRY ROUTINES	MANAGEMENT-ORIENTED RESPONSES	LEARNING-ORIENTED RESPONSES
Where am I going in my learning?	What am I expected to do? When is this due? Where are the materials for the project? What do I have to do to get an A? How many points is this worth? Who is in my group?	What are the learning intentions and success criteria? In what ways are you expected to demonstrate your understanding? In what ways can you showcase your understanding during this project?
Where am I now in my learning?	How many points is this worth? How do I get a better score? When does this need to be turned in?	What success criteria have I met? What prior knowledge do I have relative to the learning intentions? Review the rubric and identify where you are relative to the learning intention.
What next steps am I going to take in my learning?	Do I have opportunities to get a better score? Is there extra credit?	Having reviewed your current progress, what are potential next steps to improve your learning? What are ways to showcase your understanding of the learning to others?
How do I improve my learning and that of others?	Who am I going to work with in the future? How did I do relative to others?	In what ways are you finding the teacher's instruction, teacher and peer feedback, and your own learning strategies effective?' How have you supported others in their learning? What do you see as potential next steps?
Reflection	What is the percentage of information provided and shared that falls into these categories? How does this analysis differ from the past? What worked? What are areas you see for growth?	
Next Steps	What next steps do you think are required to improve the learning in the classroom?	

 Available for download at **us.corwin.com/rigorouspblbydesign** under the "Preview" tab

The Know/Need to Know list is a common tool for identifying student under-standing and areas of need (see below for further information and examples). The list can be further delineated into surface, deep, and transfer levels as well as extended to include next steps. The following activity provides three versions of a Know/Need to Know from a student using the list as he progressed through a project. The first example shows the initial layout of the list. The second and third examples illustrate how the student moved from surface to deep to transfer understanding. For additional information on the Know/Need to Know list, please use an online search engine to find the blog post titled *Putting the Know in Need to Know* (McDowell, 2013).

Here are a few steps to consider when you are using the Know/Need to Know strategy in the classroom:

1. Break the Know/Need to Know list down into the surface-, deep-, and transfer-level progressions.

2. Add an additional column for next steps for learners.

3. Post the list in the classroom for students across classes to review.

INITIAL KNOW/NEED TO KNOW TEMPLATE

TEMPLATE WITH SURFACE AND DEEP INFORMATION SUBMITTED

	K	NTK	NEXT STEPS
SURFACE	I know... — what a protein is — what a ribosome is	What is transcription? what is translation?	① Develop an outline ② Review resources
DEEP	Proteins are made in ribosomes	How do they relate?	③ create a concept map ④ Attend a workshop on protein synthesis
TRANSFER			

TEMPLATE WITH TRANSFER INFORMATION SUBMITTED

	K	NTK	NEXT STEPS
SURFACE	I know... — what a protein is — what a ribosome is	What is transcription? what is translation?	① Develop an outline ② Review resources
DEEP	Proteins are made in ribosomes	How do they relate?	③ create a concept map ④ Attend a workshop on protein synthesis
TRANSFER	Proteins are developed through protein synthesis (transcription / translation) + this process can be disrupted	How can △'s influence protein synthesis?	⑤ Build knowledge on HIV ⑥ connect to protein synthesis

NEXT STEPS

- Develop workshops at the surface, deep, and transfer level. Identify key instructional, learning, and feedback strategies that would make a substantial impact at surface, deep, and transfer levels. Include on your project template.

- Map workshops on a project calendar.

- Begin using the Know/Need to Know list to identify student prior knowledge and to clarify student surface-, deep-, and transfer-level questions.

- Come up with three ways you will infuse the following four questions in your classroom:

  Where am I going in my learning?

  Where am I now in my learning?

  What next steps am I going to take in my learning?

  How do I improve my learning and that of others?

CHAPTER 5

Design Shift III: Culture
Knowing and Acting on Impact Collectively

A culture is the result of common learning experiences.

—Clayton Christensen & Kristin Shu (2006)

In the early 2000s, an interesting phenomenon occurred at Napa New Tech High School. Several students transferred from the school to neighboring comprehensive high schools citing they wanted to "be with their friends," be "left alone," and go to an institution where "it was easier to get the A." Almost every one of those students came back within six months because after being away, they realized that everyone at New Tech cared deeply about them as people and as learners. When visiting successful schools that have a culture similar to New Tech, observers immediately identify the "culture" of the classroom or school at large. The "feeling" of the school is identified as "professional," "respectful," and "engaging." They notice the relationships between various community members; teacher to teacher, teacher to student, student to student being strikingly different from their own school experiences. They notice the language, general disposition, and routines that are used between various community members. They notice the compassion each community member has for one another. They also notice the vulnerability learners express in their own thoughts and inchoate ideas, how they are open and ready to receive and offer feedback in a way that is "soft on people and hard on content." They notice that students possess a level of advocacy for themselves and others and are confident in themselves as learners.

In my own experience as a teacher at New Tech, tour groups would walk into my classroom and be caught off guard by the intoxicatingly visceral experience of student relationships and advocacy for sharing ideas, expressing themselves, listening to others, and engaging in respectful dialogue and conflict. Two waves of surprise usually hit visiting educators: First they noted how drastically different the environment was from their own experience as a student and what they were experiencing in their current school setting. The second realization was that the culture was systematic and pervasive. There was a "community of practice." This community valued and embraced error, understood that problem- and project-based learning was a way of solving problems and making decisions at all levels of the organization, and considered collaboration to be an asset for learning because it provided people with an opportunity to listen, understand, debate, compromise, and solve challenges.

What tour groups didn't immediately recognize was the intentional design of how such a culture was put into place, maintained, and improved over time. Interestingly, many people walked away with a gap between what they observed and what needed to be done in their own school. Many observers looked for concrete, tangible solutions to close the gap. Some argued that they needed to get new furniture, put in Smart Boards, change the schedule, change the grading program, or install a project-based learning methodology; these solutions all reflected a quick fix mentality. However, such solutions have a low probability of creating the feeling and the relationships observed in the New Tech environment. The culture was intentionally designed with Question 4 in mind, *How do I improve my learning and that of others?* New Tech established core tenets of being vulnerable with others in learning (i.e., trust), understanding and appreciating differences through actions (i.e., respect), and taking ownership over individual and collective actions (i.e., responsibility). To operationalize these tenets, New Tech established routines (or protocols) and norms (or agreements) that valued a growth mindset, assessment-capable learning, and collaboration. As a result, students formed strong relationships with their peers and teachers and established a belief system and set of tools to persevere when engaging in challenging content and situations. The culture also provided the opportunity for students to be learning resources for one another and to take ownership over their learning.

Several years after I left the New Tech classroom, I had the opportunity to witness a school that designed a culture that *centered* their efforts on ensuring students (or *learners* as they are called) focused on being learning resources for one another and taking ownership over their learning. Students at Stonefields School in New Zealand had developed a command over how they learned (i.e., what strategies appeared to enhance their learning), what they learned (i.e., their current performance in relation to learning intentions and success criteria), and what they needed to do next in their learning (i.e., how to gain resources, seek feedback, or work with others to move forward). Learners had developed a "learning voice" and had a language, skill set, and disposition to actively engage with other students and teachers in the learning process. Learners could actually discuss the process of failing, why it was important, and how to navigate the process to succeed. Learners also had choice in what steps they needed to take to improve and how to support others. This level of voice and choice was built by design across the school community to ensure learners were confident and competent in their learning.

The confidence in learning attributes (assessment capabilities, growth mindset, and collaboration) found in New Tech and Stonefields can be, by design, integrated and developed in any classroom culture. This chapter focuses on specific actions teachers can take in a project-based classroom (or any classroom) to cultivate student confidence. Such actions should ensure that teachers create an inviting space for students to talk about their learning and support others in their learning (or setting the conditions). Additionally, teachers should craft a language whereby learners can discuss and monitor their learning (or voice). Finally, teachers should use strategies for building students' capacity to make choices to improve their own learning. Over time, these actions activate students as owners of their own learning and as resources for one another, resulting a substantial impact on learning.

DEVELOPING A CULTURE OF CONFIDENCE

To enable all students to have voice and choice in their learning and support others in their learning, teachers must focus on the following question: *How do I improve my learning and that of others?* This text offers the following four steps to address that question:

Step 1: Establish agreements and protocols that focus all students on learning.

Step 2: Provide tools for students to determine their level of progress and proficiency.

Step 3: Create the conditions for students to engage with failure in their learning.

Step 4: Establish processes for students to offer, receive, and use feedback to improve learning.

Step 1: Establish Agreements and Protocols That Focus All Students on Learning

The process of addressing *How do I improve my learning and that of others?* begins by setting the conditions within the classroom to ensure students and teachers are respected, hold one another accountable for learning, and trust each another in their learning. Healthy communities have explicit agreements (i.e., norms) that articulate behavioral expectations and protocols that assist in structuring conversations, decision making, and problem solving. Agreements and protocols are strategies that shape the very language and actions of the school and continually reinforce the outcomes expected within the community; the outcomes of confidence and competence (see Figure 5.1 for a specific definition and example of an agreement and protocol). Agreements are shared commitments to how people within a community behave. Agreements are transparent, understandable, and are often used to

FIGURE 5.1 Student Learning: Sample Agreement and Protocol

AGREEMENT	PROTOCOL
Shared commitment on actions	Specific process on how to act
Example I will explain my rationale when I express my opinion.	**Example** Sharing personal performance data Step 1: Share data and provide only facts (no inferences). Step 2: Share inferences drawn and rationale for inferences. Step 3: Solicit clarifying questions from others. Step 4: Identify inferences from others. Step 5: Create next steps.

redirect community members who infringe or violate such commitments. Protocols are specific processes for how to handle decisions in a learning-centered culture (see Figure 5.2 for sample agreements and protocols).

When cultures actively use agreements and protocols that are built on confidence, people are more likely to solve challenging problems. As Clayton Christensen and Kristin Shu write (2006),

> [M]embers [of a culture] share a significant number of common experiences in successfully addressing external and internal problems. Because of these experiences, over time this group of people will have formed a shared view of the way that the world surrounding them works, and of the methods for problem solving that will be effective in that world. This shared view of the world has led to the formation of basic assumptions and beliefs that have worked well enough and long enough to be taken for granted. These basic assumptions and beliefs are learned responses to the problems that the group has encountered as its members have tried to work together to survive in the face of challenges. (p. 1)

When designing and implementing projects, it is paramount to establish agreements and protocols that focus students on understanding and improving learning. Certain protocols and agreements can create the conditions for students to feel comfortable expressing their voice (i.e., discussing their performance and giving and receiving feedback) and choice (i.e., strategies they use and the means to convey success) in the classroom. Ultimately, leveraging voice (being able to talk about their learning) and choice (being able to make decisions about next steps in learning) provides students with

FIGURE 5.2 Classroom Culture: Sample Agreement and Protocols

AGREEMENT	PROTOCOL
Shared commitment on actions	Specific process on how to act

Example
 	
Teachers and learners will
 	
• give and receive feedback that is "soft on people and hard on content."
 	
• use questions to address potential conflicts, explore ideas, and test assumptions.
 	
• explain important words and provide specific examples when needed.
 	
• share everything.
	Example
	
	Teachers and learners will demonstrate collective agreements by using the following protocols:
	
	• Protocol 2.1, What? So What? Now What?
	
	• Protocol 5.1, Critical Friends Team (CFT)
	
	• Protocol 5.2, Learning Dilemma
	
	• Protocol 5.3, Constructivist Listening
	
	• NSRF Protocol Save the Last Word for Me
	
	  ○ See Chapter 2 and Chapter 5 activities for protocols.
	
	  ○ See National School Reform Faculty (NSRF) for additional protocols (www.nsrfharmony.org).

the level of autonomy needed to take full responsibility over their own learning over time.

Established agreements and protocols must be directly modeled by teachers and embedded within classroom and schoolwide projects. Such agreements and protocols set the conditions in which to articulate what is expected and how to respond when agreements or protocols are honored or violated. The mantra here is "model, model, model" and is likened to the adage "do unto others as you would do unto yourself." Everyone uses particular actions that enable students to be confident in their learning and develop competence through a culture that solves problems from a basis in trust, respect, and responsibility. These agreements and protocols are modeled every day. As Andrew Larson (personal communication, July 17, 2012), a teacher at Signature Academy New Tech stated, "You must keep your finger on the pulse of culture every second of every day. There is no pause, no break. This is the critical feature to a collaborative, problem solving learning community."

Once agreements and protocols are established and the conditions for learning are set, students have the opportunity to develop a language of learning (or voice) as a means to discuss their progress and proficiency; face failure or stagnation in their learning; monitor progress; showcase performance; and give, receive, and use feedback to improve learning.

Bobby Thompson
Principal, Triton Central Middle School
Fairland, IN
www.nwshelbyschools.org/middleschool

Our middle school and high school have been using PBL practices for eight years. Our district was looking for a teaching model that would allow our students to gain real-life experiences and build skill sets that would allow them to compete in a global market in the 21st century. Our research proved to us that using PBL would allow us to meet the requirements of state standardized testing and give our students the best opportunities to build qualities that the workforce is demanding, such as collaboration and a work ethic.

A few thoughts come to mind for schools that are attempting full-scale PBL implementation.

1. First, I would make sure that the district's culture is ready for this kind of teaching method. We found that culture was the most important facet of successful PBL implementation.

2. Second, a corporation must be ready to provide many hours of training and follow-up coaching to allow teachers the opportunity to grow in a pedagogy that isn't widely taught in teacher preparation courses.

3. Third, I would encourage the school community to be patient with the process of a full-scale implementation as it will take time for teachers to perfect this teaching method. Have an understanding that teachers may F.A.I.L. (First Attempt in Learning) at times, and there will need to be planned moments of reflection and re-teaching. This freedom to fail will allow teachers to create really robust projects that will pay huge dividends to students. During the implementation, we realized that not all teachers have the desire or skill set to successfully teach using a PBL model. We have, therefore, used our judgment regarding which teachers to place in our PBL classrooms. We want teachers to use their strengths, and if they have strengths other than PBL, we encourage them to exercise those strengths so that we can provide the best learning experience possible for our students.

To be quite honest, we have not seen drastic changes in the measurable things such as attendance and graduation rates because ours have been consistently in the higher ranges; however, we have received tremendous feedback from our alumni and visitors to our schools. Our graduates are providing us feedback that they are excelling in certain areas compared to their peers, such as in interviews and leading successful group projects. Additionally, we consistently hear from our visitors how impressed they are with how well our students communicate, self-advocate, and express themselves. In my opinion, this is a direct reflection of the opportunities PBL provides to develop and grow student's skills in these areas.

When I think about designing my school around PBL, quite honestly, I like being different. Thirteen percent of our student population chooses to come to our schools from other districts, because they like our schools and what we do differently than their home school district. They like the culture of our buildings, and their parents like the different learning opportunities our schools offer their children.

One thing I would do differently if I were to do another PBL implementation is that I would not force teachers into using this model. Dictating that everyone use the PBL model caused an ineffective implementation where we ended up focusing on things other than students' learning. I found that there are teachers who will not or cannot use this method effectively to deliver content.

Something I still struggle with is our team-taught classes. I have found that after about three years of team-teaching, the relationships between the teachers start to deteriorate. This phenomenon is contrary to what I thought would happen. I thought time would make them more effective, and they would learn more about each other so that they can be more dynamic. They do indeed learn more about each other, but this knowledge usually leads to frustration and bitterness. I am working on strategies to keep this from happening or ways to rotate teachers so that we do not hit this tipping point of frustration or bitterness.

Step 2: Provide Tools for Students to Determine Their Level of Progress and Proficiency

To develop confidence, students need a way to discuss and track their own learning. To ensure students have the tools to do so, teachers should structure time during class for students to share their learning data and work with others to develop a collective understanding of performance. Similar to professional learning communities for teachers, students need time to meet with partners or in teams to share their own proficiency and progress and understand, reflect, and contribute to the learning of others.

To establish a language of learning, teachers may want to consider the approach Stonefields School uses to ensure students have a clear understanding of their learning. Students at Stonefields School have created colloquialisms to describe levels of learning (surface, deep, transfer). When a student is engaging in new content (surface level) they state they are "building knowledge." As learners begin to go deeper in their learning and are comparing and contrasting ideas, they are "making meaning." Finally, as students develop the ability to transfer or extend their understanding in different situations, they are "applying understanding." This language of learning is pervasive at Stonefields School, and students continuously use the language to understand their level of learning. Figure 5.3 provides an illustration of a language of learning that students could use to discuss their level of understanding. Figure 5.4 provides tools to assist teachers in developing a language of learning for learners.

Even when the conditions and a common language are established, students need to have a common way to discuss their progress and proficiency. One viable strategy is to delineate performance levels that are deemed proficient and to create a standard measure of adequate growth in learning over time. One suggestion is for students and teachers to use a 0.0–4.0 scale to match the learning levels reviewed in this book (surface, deep, and transfer) and the

FIGURE 5.3 A Language of Learning

UNKNOWN	SURFACE	DEEP	TRANSFER
Need support	*Building knowledge*	*Making meaning*	*Applying understanding*
The students are unclear on expectations or unclear on relationship between what they know and what is expected.	The student is working to understand single and multiple ideas or skills.	The student is working to relate ideas or skills together.	The student is applying ideas or skills in various situations.

SOURCE: Hook & Cassé (2013).

 Available for download at **us.corwin.com/rigorouspblbydesign** under the "Preview" tab

FIGURE 5.4 Tools for Developing a Language of Learning

BUILD RUBRICS	Teachers build clear and concise rubrics that outline success criteria to progression levels. A list of tasks may be included as representative ways for learners to demonstrate their understanding.
THE MATCHING GAME	Learners are given three pieces of learner work and have to identify whether each piece meets the building-knowledge, making-meaning, or applying-understanding level of the rubric.
CREATING VISUAL MAPS OF PROGRESSION	Teachers provide tangible symbols of progression (such as a staircase) and illustrate where students are in their learning journey.
ESTABLISHING LANGUAGE ACTIVITIES FOR LEARNERS AND PARENTS	Learners and parents attend school and take part in activities that are linked to surface-, deep-, and transfer-level learning. Learners spend time talking with parents about the different levels of learning and where they are in their own learning.

language of learning discussed earlier (building knowledge, making meaning, and applying understanding). In addition, students and teachers should designate a proficiency level (such as 3.0 or above) to be within the zone of success for students. This designation would allow educators and students to clearly delineate student performance levels and thus consider specific, targeted support.

To assist in this effort, this text recommends that teachers create a rubric that uses the language of learning for each level of success criteria. A rubric is a common tool that aligns the progression levels of knowledge and skill along a common scale (see Figure 5.5 as an example).

If rubrics are to be used, the recommendation here is to depict only success criteria for each learning intention and remove any specific tasks or contexts that are related to the project. By removing context, learners will have a better understanding of learning intention expectations and will have an easier time engaging in transfer-level work. Additionally, by removing tasks, students have the opportunity to work with teachers to select (i.e., student choice) tasks that best represent their understanding. Often rubrics are used for scoring and grading purposes. The recommendation here is to use a simplified four-point scale divided into half-point increments to better estimate progress. Figure 5.6 integrates a scoring schema into the template shown on Figure 5.5. Figures 5.7 and 5.8 provide sample rubrics that align with learning intentions and success criteria.

FIGURE 5.5 Sample Rubric

One suggestion is to use the following rubric labels:

- **Level 0–1: With Support:** Unclear on expectations and unable to meet surface-level expectations with support from teachers or peers.

- **Level 2: Building Knowledge or Skills (Surface):** Describes outcomes that require the learner to identify or describe a single fact or idea. The learner lists or describes several relevant factors, ideas, or skills, but has made no connection between them.

- **Level 3: Making Meaning or Connecting Skills (Deep):** Describes outcomes where the learner must make connections and relate between several relevant facts or skills.

- **Level 4: Applying Understanding or Skill (Transfer):** Describes outcomes where the learner has applied relational understanding or skills to some other concept, theory, or context.

SUCCESS CRITERIA	SCORE
Transfer *Applying Understanding*	Met transfer expectations Partially met transfer expectations
Deep *Making Meaning*	Met deep expectations Partially met deep expectations
Surface *Building Knowledge*	Met single-/multiple-level expectations Partial success with single-/multiple-level expectations
With Support	With instructional support, student met single-/multiple-level and relational expectations. With instructional support, student met single-/multiple-level expectations. With instructional support, student has not met single-/multiple-level expectations.

Available for download at **us.corwin.com/rigorouspblbydesign** under the "Preview" tab

FIGURE 5.6 Sample Rubric With Scoring Schema

SUCCESS CRITERIA	SCORE	
Transfer *Applying Understanding*	4.0	Met transfer expectations
	3.5	Partially met transfer expectations
Deep *Making Meaning*	3.0	Met deep expectations
	2.5	Partially met deep expectations
Surface *Building Knowledge*	2.0	Met single-/multiple-level expectations
	1.5	Partial success with single-/multiple-level expectations
With Support	1.0	With instructional support, student met single-/multiple-level and relational expectations.
	0.5	With instructional support, student met single-/multiple-level expectations.
	0.0	With instructional support, student has not met single-/multiple-level expectations.

FIGURE 5.7 Rubric Example in English Language Arts

Standard/Outcome: Students will initiate and participate effectively in a range of collaborative discussions (one on one, in groups, and teacher led) with diverse partners on grade-appropriate topics, texts, and issues, building on others' ideas and expressing their own clearly and persuasively (CCSS.ELA-Literacy.SL. 11–12.1).

SUCCESS CRITERIA	SCORE	
Transfer *Applying Understanding*	4.0	I can use conversational strategies in various contexts.
	3.5	I can use conversational strategies but still struggle in certain contexts.
Deep *Making Meaning*	3.0	I can connect preparation, engagement, and leveraging strategies to engage with others.
	2.5	I understand conversational strategies and am working toward relating the strategies together.

(Continued)

FIGURE 5.7 (Continued)

SUCCESS CRITERIA	SCORE	
Surface *Building Knowledge*	2.0	I can • use evidence from texts and other research on topics or issues to stimulate a thoughtful, well-reasoned exchange of ideas. • respond to questions that probe reasoning and evidence. • respond thoughtfully to diverse perspectives and prompt further dialogue.
	1.5	I can use a range of conversational strategies in the making meaning section when prompted and supported by the teacher. I'm still working on using collaborative strategies.
With Support	1.0	With help from the teacher, I meet the building knowledge success criteria.
	0.5	The teacher provides me with significant support to meet building knowledge criteria.
	0.0	I'm still struggling with understanding the learning intention and success criteria.

In addition to determining student proficiency ranges, teachers and learners need to understand the paramount importance of utilizing learner growth over time to determine progress and to determine instructional and learning strategy efficacy. Paul Barton (2006) argues, "The end goal should be reaching a standard for how much growth we expect during a school year in any particular subject (p. 30)." This growth standard has been developed within John Hattie's work on effect size and in longitudinal databases such as the Progress in International Reading Literacy Study (PIRLS); the Program for International Student Assessment (PISA); the Trends in International Mathematics and Science Study (TIMSS); the National Assessment of Educational Progress (NAEP); the National Assessment Program—Literacy and Numeracy (NAPLAN; Hattie, 2009, 2011).

As stated previously, Hattie's research indicates that the average effect of all variables on student achievement is 0.40. He argues,

FIGURE 5.8 Sample Rubric for Science

	SCORE
Transfer • I can apply my understanding of how various factors may influence protein creation in different contexts.	3.5–4.0
Deep • I understand how transcription and translation relate to one another to create proteins.	2.5–3.0
Surface • I can define transcription, translation, RNA, and DNA and understand these concepts are involved in creating proteins.	1.5–2.0
Instructional Support	0.0–1.0

Setting the bar at an effect size of $d = 0.0$ is so low as to be dangerous. We need to be more discriminating. For any particular intervention to be considered worthwhile, it needs to show an improvement in student learning of at least an average gain—that is, an effect size of at least 0.40. The $d = 0.40$ is what I referred to in *Visible Learning* as the hinge-point (or h-point) for identifying what is and what is not effective. (Hattie, 2012, pp. 2–3)

Average knowledge or skill gains are also a consideration for a system to serve as a growth standard for student progress. As Robert Marzano and Timothy Waters (2009) report, "a district might set a nonnegotiable goal that every student must progress at least 0.5 scale points each quarter for specific topics in reading, writing, and mathematics" (p. 43). For example, let's suppose that a teacher team developed a growth standard of 0.5 scale points for all students. Using Figure 5.8, let's imagine that students started their project with a score of 2.0 (meaning they have met surface-level understanding). At or near the conclusion of the project, the students took an assessment and scored at the 3.5 level (meaning they have met many, though not all, transfer-level criteria) indicating a growth of 1.5 scaled points. If the goal for the teacher team was to have students grow at least 0.5 scaled points a quarter, then these students are clearly on their way given their growth in the project.

The use of standard growth and attainment of designated levels of learning provides individual teachers, teams, and learners a high level of flexibility in selecting and using assessments, scoping and sequencing outcomes across a class, and identifying project context and duration. This flexibility reduces the need and desire for strict pacing guides and unit-by-unit agreements by teachers. This is of paramount importance in the PBL classroom, as projects may vary in duration, 21st century skill expectations, project context, and overall course scope and sequence based on the overall philosophy of approaching a discipline; or, in the case of integrated projects or courses, approaching integrated disciplines.

By creating assessment instruments (i.e., rubrics) that focus on success criteria aligned with specific learning intentions as opposed to tasks or context-laden information, assessment instruments may be used across projects and across schools. Specifically, multiple teachers and students could implement different projects, tasks, and assessments while simultaneously and accurately measuring student progress and proficiency on learning intentions and success criteria using the same rubric(s). Moreover, in this way, students would have the opportunity to have choice in how they demonstrate their understanding independent of any and all tasks and contexts (see Marzano, 2009). A rubric combined with a language of learning provides the opportunity for students to advocate for ways to demonstrate their understanding, identify next steps, and analyze ways to apply their understanding in various contexts—the essence of voice and choice.

> A rubric combined with a language of learning provides the opportunity for students to advocate for ways to demonstrate their understanding, identify next steps, and analyze ways to apply their understanding in various contexts—the essence of voice and choice.

To effectively and efficiently review and respond to learning data, teachers and learners need to collectively understand and agree to proficiency ranges from their designated learning levels and progress-based reference points (see Figure 5.9 for a visual representation of progress and proficiency levels). Figure 5.10 illustrates proficiency matrices that

FIGURE 5.9   Progress and Proficiency Levels

Quadrant II	Quadrant I
Low Progress	High Progress
High Proficiency	High Proficiency

Quadrant III	Quadrant IV
Low Progress	High Progress
Low Proficiency	Low Proficiency

FIGURE 5.10 Student Progress and Proficiency Matrix

	LIMITED PROGRESS (0.00–0.39; OR GAINS LESS THAN 0.5)	SUBSTANTIAL PROGRESS (0.40+; GAINS ABOVE 0.5)
PROFICIENT (DEEP TO TRANSFER) 2.50–4.0	Quadrant II • Instructional change • Change in learning strategy • Review type of feedback	Quadrant I • Celebrate success • Set new challenge • Reflect on instructional and learning strategies that move learning forward • Reflect on types of feedback
NOT YET PROFICIENT (SURFACE TO DEEP) 0.0–2.25	Quadrant III • Instructional change • Change in learning strategy • Review type of feedback	Quadrant IV • Additional time and celebrate success • Reflect on instructional and learning strategies that move learning forward

students and teachers may utilize to understand student performance. Each quadrant is explained below.

Quadrant I: High Progress and High Proficiency

In *Quadrant I*, students have met key outcomes and showed substantial growth throughout the learning process. The *Quadrant I* performance category illuminates strategies that have successfully advanced students to levels of mastery. In addition, *Quadrant I* requires teachers and students to consider new outcomes to explore or new challenges to enhance learning.

Quadrant II: Low Progress and High Proficiency

In *Quadrant II*, students are showing levels of proficiency, yet are indicating limited growth in learning. Similar to *Quadrant III*, instructional, feedback, and learning strategies to support student learning at the 3.0 and 4.0 level require examination and potential augmentation. Instructional strategies that may be useful at the 2.5–3.0 level revolve around reviewing content (demonstration, summaries), practicing and deepening knowledge (perspective analysis), examining similarities and differences (Venn diagram), and examining errors in reasoning (identifying errors and misinformation; Marzano, 2012). At the 3.5–4.0 level range, strategies to advance student learning might include organization of students (cooperative learning), engagement (problem solving), and providing resources and guidance (probing support).

Quadrant III: Low Progress and Low Proficiency

In *Quadrant III,* individual students are identified as having not yet met proficiency (NYP) and not progressing at the established growth rate or average gains for a particular learning outcome. Instructional, feedback, and learning strategy augmentations are considered a key approach for enhancing student learning in this performance category. Instructional recommendations are offered that have a "high probability" of yielding effective growth at the 0.0–2.0 level. For example, Marzano (2007) identifies numerous strategies to support students in identifying critical information (e.g., visual activities, tone of voice, gestures, body positions), organizing students to interact with new knowledge (e.g., group norms, jigsaws), previewing new content (e.g., skimming, overt linkages), chunking content (e.g., using preassessment data to vary the size of each chunk, presenting content in small chunks), elaborate (e.g., elaborative interrogation), record and represent (e.g., graphic organizers), and reflections (e.g., exit slips). Beyond pedagogical strategies, the focus on content and instructional routines may be considered, such as the utilization of formative assessment practices (e.g., clarifying learning intentions, tracking progress, offering feedback) or establishing and maintaining the classroom climate (e.g., procedures and rules, physical layout of the classroom). These instructional routines, as defined by Marzano (2007, 2012) provide a broader level of consideration that is commonly recommended when a substantial portion of students are grouped into Quadrant II and Quadrant III. Additional strategies that enhance engagement, such as recognizing and acknowledging adherence to classroom rules and procedures, establishing and maintaining effective relationships, and communicating high expectations may be considered to enhance growth in learning (Marzano, 2007).

Quadrant IV: High Progress and Low Proficiency

In *Quadrant IV,* students have met an acceptable growth rate yet have not met proficiency. Additional time considerations are deemed appropriate in this performance category, while at the same time, cataloging instructional strategies for future use, as certain instructional strategies were considered successful within the classroom and school context in enhancing student learning over time. This is an optimal time to support students in reflecting on the efficacy of learning strategies and for teachers to review the efficacy of their feedback.

Once a student's progress and proficiency is understood, teachers and students can respond effectively. For example, suppose teachers and students conducted a pre- and postassessment based on a 0.0–4.0 scale, with an established proficiency range and growth rate. Figure 5.11 details the performance of 28 students assessed on a particular outcome. Figure 5.12 illustrates the group and individual effect sizes (i.e., means for measuring growth over time) as well as the proficiency level for each student. Figure 5.10 highlights the students who fall within a certain quadrant: proficiency range (not yet proficient would be 0.0–1.5, and proficient levels are 2.0–4.0) and a growth criterion (0.40 hinge-point). From these data, teachers and students could work individually and within teams to identify next steps (see Figure 4.1 for ideas on instructional-, feedback-, and learning-based strategies) to enhance student learning.

To summarize, the utilization of growth/progress and attainment/proficiency data to gauge learner proficiency is important for students and teachers to understand performance levels and ultimately to identify next steps in the teaching and learning process. By knowing performance levels, teachers can target necessary interventions for all learners, assess efficacy of current teaching practices, and mobilize individual and collective efforts to celebrate success and improve current teaching practice. Learners can reflect on their own learning strategies and identify what next steps they need to take to improve. They also have a language tied to the levels of

> By knowing performance levels, teachers can target necessary interventions for all learners, assess efficacy of current teaching practices, and mobilize individual and collective efforts to celebrate success and improve current teaching practice.

FIGURE 5.11 Pre/Post Proficiency

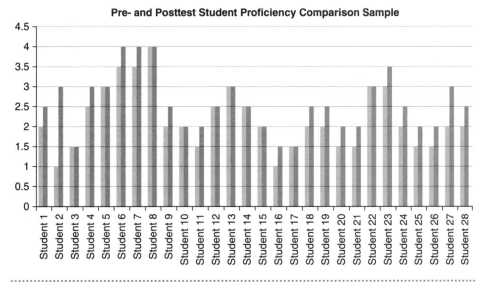

SOURCE: Lynn Christofferson, 2014, Tamalpais Union High School District, Larkspur, CA.

FIGURE 5.12   Individual and Group Effect Size Data

	PRETEST	POSTTEST	DIFFERENCE	SPREAD/SD (AVERAGE)	GROUP EFFECT SIZE	STUDENT EFFECT SIZE
MEAN SCORES	2.18	2.57				
DIFFERENCE			0.39			
SPREAD/SD	0.77	0.72				
AVERAGE SD				0.74		
EFFECT SIZE					0.528	
Student 1	2	2.5				0.68
Student 2	1	3				2.70
Student 3	1.5	1.5				0.00
Student 4	2.5	3				0.68
Student 5	3	3				0.00
Student 6	3.5	4				0.68
Student 7	3.5	4				0.68
Student 8	4	4				0.00
Student 9	2	2.5				0.68
Student 10	2	2				0.00
Student 11	1.5	2				0.68
Student 12	2.5	2.5				0.00
Student 13	3	3				0.00
Student 14	2.5	2.5				0.00
Student 15	2	2				0.00
Student 16	1	1.5				0.68
Student 17	1.5	1.5				0.00
Student 18	2	2.5				0.68
Student 19	2	2.5				0.68
Student 20	1.5	2				0.68
Student 21	1.5	2				0.68
Student 22	3	3				0.00
Student 23	3	3.5				0.68
Student 24	2	2.5				0.68
Student 25	1.5	2				0.68
Student 26	1.5	2				0.68
Student 27	2	3				1.35
Student 28	2	2.5				0.68

SOURCE: Lynn Christofferson, 2014, Tamalpais Union High School District, Larkspur, CA.

learning, which are directly aligned with success criteria that are mapped on a rubric. This level of alignment provides students with the support needed to discuss their progress and proficiency. Figure 5.13 provides teachers with a few strategies to support students in tracking and discussing their own learning.

Ultimately, the analysis of proficiency and progress data should provide teachers and students with the information necessary to identify appropriate next steps in the learning and teaching process. During this time, the role of the teacher is paramount in monitoring student team dialogue to ensure that the conversation is focused on learning. Unfortunately, research has shown that students and teachers in the PBL environment are often unprepared to navigate tricky feedback discussions especially when disagreement is afoot (McDowell, 2009). Theresa Ochoa and Jennifer Meta Robinson (2005) declared, "Inadequate reasoning, negotiation, and reflection that easily capitulate to an untested opinion remain problematic" (p. 9) in PBL environments. Furthermore, Ochoa et al. (2001) concluded that groups do not constructively negotiate opinions and rarely, if ever, arrive at a collective opinion. In the PBL environment, teachers who were recognized as having the right beliefs either lacked the actual behaviors that prompted and facilitated

FIGURE 5.13 Supporting Learners in Tracking and Discussing Their Own Progress

GOOGLE SHEETS	Teachers submit to each student a Google spreadsheet with a list of learning standards, associated rubrics, and a space to provided notes. The teacher has access rights to view the learner's tracking. The teacher and the learner meet to discuss the learner's reporting and to craft potential next steps.
BRING MY EVIDENCE	Learners meet in small groups of three to five and share a piece of evidence they have to illustrate their level of proficiency against a rubric. Each learner takes turns describing her work and why it represents a level of proficiency. Then the rest of the group asks questions that further the learner's thinking on her proficiency level. At the conclusion of the activity, the teacher asks for the main questions that were brought forward from each group to identify potential next steps in the teaching and learning process.
THE MATCHING GAME	Learners are given three pieces of work belonging to a student, and they have to identify whether the pieces meet surface-, deep-, and/or transfer-level success criteria depicted on the scoring rubric.

appropriate dialogue or failed to intervene adequately on issues related to learning (McDowell, 2009). However, by using agreements and protocols (as shown above), providing tools to enable learners to develop a language of learning, establishing a common conception of progress and proficiency, and using tools that align with learning intentions and success criteria, these conversations may be more impactful in the future.

Step 3: Create the Conditions for Students to Engage With Failure in Their Learning

To further support students in developing their confidence in learning, teachers should consider establishing the conditions necessary for students to discuss and engage with failure. When students are finding difficulty at the surface, deep, and transfer levels of learning, they need to have a way to convey this experience in a natural and positive light. By leveraging the language of learning discussed in the last section, teachers may work with students to discuss how the process of learning often follows a nonlearner process. One student (learner) at Stonefields School describes the learning process as "unpredictable" or nonlinear and articulates how often students may have to revisit core concepts at the surface (or building knowledge) level of learning to deepen their understanding. When learners understand that this process is a natural part of learning, they are more likely to convey to others their level of learning and admit when they are stuck in their learning.

One way of conveying this idea of failure is through the use of the Learning Challenge (see Figure 5.14). Learners at Stonefields use the term *learning pit* to describe the point at which they get stuck or confused in their learning. Tools such as the language of learning help them seek resources, gain feedback, reflect on their learning, and review data to gain clarity and move forward. The Learning Challenge comes from James Nottingham's (2010) work, which articulates the idea that when learners reach a level of cognitive disequilibrium (i.e., "They are stuck") they have to seek resources, feedback, and direct guidance to move out of a state of confusion (i.e., the pit).

The pit is critical to learning and plays a significant role in PBL. For example, during the project launch, learners are introduced to the entry event, which provides the scenario of the project, the driving question they need to answer, the specific task and underlying content, as well as expectations for their learning. During this time, teachers ask learners to identify what they know related to the project and questions (or "need to knows") they may have about the project. Furthermore, teachers provide a preassessment to glean further insight into the knowledge base of students and what is expected. Teachers illustrate this perceived gap between what learners as a class know and need to know, creating a collective learning pit. Over time, students get out of the pit by answering the need–to-know questions at the surface level and then fall back in again as they move to more complex learning goals (see example of a Know/Need to Know list in Activity 4.4).

FIGURE 5.14 The Learning Challenge

SOURCE: Used with permission from James Nottingham.

FIGURE 5.15   Engaging in the Pit Activities

Students should consider the following questions:

- **Surface Level:** What learning strategies will support me in understanding foundational knowledge (e.g., facts, vocabulary terms) related to learning outcomes?

- **Deep Level:** What learning strategies will support me in connecting and contrasting ideas? What generalizations and principles can be drawn from these ideas?

- **Transfer Level:** What learning strategies support me in applying the learning outcomes to project expectations?

SIGNALING	When a learner enters the pit, he use a signal (green cup for GO!) and looks for a learner with a red cup (waiting to go into the pit) to discuss their confusion. The two learners plot out a path to navigate out of the pit starting with identifying where the learners are going in their learning, where they are, and the steps that have supported them before when in the pit. Then the learners work together to come up with a solution (e.g., ask for a workshop, seek another learner who may possess the information needed, ask for a model of what is requested).
FISHBOWL	Every learner experiences the pit, but often a public discussion and debrief of the pit are lacking. For the Fishbowl exercise, the teacher puts five chairs in the middle of the classroom while the learners circle and face the chairs. The teacher then sits down (at least the first time) on one of the chairs as do three other students. One chair remains empty for a student from the circle to come sit down and engage in the conversation. If and when a student sits down, someone has to get up (usually the teacher if the discussion is progressing). In the center of the fishbowl, there are always four occupied chairs and one empty chair. The group in the middle discusses questions such as *What does it feel like to be in the pit? How did you get out? How do you begin to get comfortable being uncomfortable? How can the classroom be more conducive to being in the pit? What are the best strategies to help learners get out and get in? What happens if you don't get in the pit? What's happening in your learning?*
	It can be up to students to come in and out of the circle independently; or, to encourage more students to participate, teachers may randomly select students' name from a jar. The teacher can call out "switch" to indicate that a student from outside the bowl sits down. To indicate which student should leave the inner circle, she can tap that student on the shoulder.

Selecting and monitoring their own learning strategies is one way learners can help themselves get out of the pit (see Figure 5.15). Similar to how a teacher identifies the best strategy for instruction, students identify the best learning strategy when they are at surface-, deep-, and transfer-level learning. Engaging students in reflecting on their current performance level, discussing their current struggles in learning, and identifying strategies that may enhance their learning supports the development of a growth mindset, assessment capabilities, and the collaboration necessary to build confidence. It is also yet another way to promote visible learning.

Step 4: Establish Processes for Students to Offer, Receive, and Use Feedback to Improve Learning

As discussed in Chapter 4, feedback is most effective when it is targeted to a student's level of understanding (surface, deep, or transfer). If teachers have established agreements and protocols that enable students and teachers to discuss learning, provided a language of learning and tools for discussing and measuring learning, developed a common set of beliefs and processes for discussing the importance of failure, then teachers and students are more likely to align feedback with the specific learning needs of students, and students are more likely to take such feedback and make improvements. Moreover, students are more likely to give accurate feedback to one another. In the Mangere Bridge School in Auckland, New Zealand, students take part in data teams to review their performance levels. Through these discussions, students receive feedback from teachers and peers, reflect on their own performance, and articulate what steps they need to take to improve. Figure 5.16 offers resources to support students and teachers in developing their feedback capacity.

FIGURE 5.16 Giving and Receiving Feedback Strategies

DIGGING DEEPER	Pair students in groups of two.
	1. Student A shares her current progress with Student B.
	2. Student B then paraphrases what he heard from Student A and suggests that they are at a certain level (surface, deep, or transfer).
	3. Student B offers suggestions on how to improve to the right level.
	4. The students then switch roles and repeat steps 1 through 3.
	5. Students report their findings to the teacher.
CRITICAL FRIENDS TEAM	See Activity 5.2, Protocol 5.1
LEARNING DILEMMA	See Activity 5.2, Protocol 5.2

CONCLUSION

A major shift in the PBL environment is to ensure that the right culture is established where learners have the knowledge and skills to develop assessment capabilities, a growth mindset, and collaborative skills. This is accomplished by specific actions including developing the right conditions in the classroom (through specific agreements and protocols), developing student voice (by establishing a language of learning, how to discuss challenge, means for monitoring progress), and developing student choice (in selecting ways to demonstrate their understanding). If the environment is not established to focus on learning, it is extremely difficult for learners to actualize a growth mindset or action set, develop the skills to be an assessment-capable learner, and create a community of assessment-capable learners through collaboration.

QUESTIONS FOR REFLECTION

- How do you know your impact? How do your students know their progress? Do they have a language of learning?

- How can you model the importance of assessment capabilities in the classroom? What agreements and protocols will support you in this transition?

- How did your understanding of student voice and student choice shift after reading this text?

- What tools do you provide and use to measure growth (progress) and proficiency? How do you and your students truly know your impact? How do you ensure a 0.40 effect size?

- What conditions do you put in place to ensure students perceive failure as an important part of their learning? How do your instructional, feedback, and assessment strategies reflect the importance of failure in learning?

- How do you provide targeted feedback to enhance student learning? How do you build student capacity to give targeted feedback and to use feedback received from peers to improve?

ACTIVITIES

Know Thy Impact

Review the performance data in this Chapter (see Figures 5.11 and 5.12) and categorize students into the four quadrants shown in Figure 5.9 and discussed in Figure 5.10. Next, answer the following questions:

> After reviewing the data in Figures 5.11 and 5.12, how would you provide instructional- and feedback-based interventions for students who fall in Quadrants I, II, III, and IV?

> How would you support students in understanding their progress and proficiency, and in determining next steps?

> After you are familiar with this data analysis, collect your own pre/post data and engage in the same process. Over time, engaging students in their own data analysis and identifying next steps will be extremely powerful in promoting the type of learning culture discussed in this chapter.

Activity 5.2 Protocols for Feedback

Select one of the following protocols to solicit feedback from your students on your project. Next, indicate to students how their feedback supported your learning and what changes, if any, you made to your project. Finally, provide opportunities for students to use these protocols with each other on their project work.

> Protocol 5.1, Critical Friends Team (CFT)

> Protocol 5.2, Learning Dilemma

> Protocol 5.3, Constructivist Listening

PROTOCOL 5.1: Critical Friends Team (CFT)

▶ The following protocol is designed to provide students and educators with specific feedback regarding a product.

Total Time: 45 minutes

Opening Moves (Introduction) (5 minutes)

- Review purpose of protocol.

- Review agreements (norms) of the team.

- Identify someone as the facilitator of the process.

- Review success criteria of product being evaluated.

Opening Presentation (5 minutes)

- The facilitator invites a student or teacher (presenter) to present the product he or she wants to have reviewed.

- The presenter provides a 2–3-minute overview of the product.

- The facilitator then invites the others to ask clarifying questions.

- The presenter provides answers to any clarifying question.

  - *This process can be much more effective when materials are provided before the CFT Review. One suggestion is to email all CFT members materials to be reviewed 72 hours before the CFT process.*

Strengths (I like) (10 minutes)

- Facilitator asks the CFT to provide feedback related to the strengths of the product.

- CFT members will begin each piece of feedback using the following stems: "I like . . . because . . . ." or "One strength is . . . because . . . ." (Rationale should be related to success criteria.)

  - *During these three sections (Strengths, Questions, and Next Steps), the presenter receiving feedback should not make any remarks and should only listen and write down notes.*

  - *The facilitator should ensure that all feedback information is documented.*

Questions (I wonder) (10 minutes)

- Facilitator asks the CFT to provide questions for the presenter to think through regarding the product.

- CFT members will begin each piece of feedback using the following stems: "I wonder if. . ." or "One question to consider includes . . . ." (Rationale should be related to success criteria.)

Next Steps (10 minutes)

- Facilitator asks the CFT to provide feedback on the suggested next steps related to the product.

- CFT members will begin each piece of feedback using the following stems: "One next step to consider is . . . ." (Rationale should be related to success criteria.)

Closing Remarks (5 minutes)

- The presenter receiving feedback has the opportunity to thank the CFT for their feedback and to provide specific next steps they will take in light of the feedback they received.

 Available for download at **us.corwin.com/rigorouspblbydesign** under the "Preview" tab

▶ The following protocol provides individuals with a structured process for students and teachers to work together to solve a problem that one person (the presenter) is facing in his or her learning. Example dilemmas including not making progress, not meeting transfer-level expectations, feeling stuck in understanding certain content, and struggling with identifying learning strategies that help a student move his or her learning forward.

Total Time: 45 minutes

Opening Moves (Introduction) (5 minutes)

- Review protocol purpose and process. Review agreements (or norms) of the team.

- Identify facilitator, presenter, and reviewers.

Statements of Dilemma (10 minutes)

- The facilitator asks the presenter to describe a learning dilemma to others. The presenter briefly explains the dilemma and addresses the following questions: *Why is this important? Why is this a dilemma? How is this a dilemma? What is causing this dilemma?* (Presenter may bring exemplars/artifacts.)

- The facilitator asks the group to pose any clarifying questions to the presenter. The presenter answers clarifying questions.

Discussing Dilemma (10 minutes)

- While the group discusses the dilemma, the presenter listens and takes notes but does not speak.

- The group discusses the dilemma. The facilitator asks the group to focus their discussion on the following questions: *What are the important facts that have emerged in this dilemma? What are the assumptions underlying the dilemma? What are potential perspectives or questions that may be of value to consider?*

Reflection From Presenter (10 minutes)

- Based on the feedback from the group, the presenter shares his or her reflections and discusses next steps.

Reflection on Process (10 minutes)

- The facilitator asks the presenter and the group the following questions: *What were the strengths in our adherence to the protocol? How could we improve our process?*

Available for download at **us.corwin.com/rigorouspblbydesign** under the "Preview" tab

PROTOCOL 5.3: Constructivist Listening

▶ The following protocol supports group members in preparing for listening in a group setting.

Total Time: 10 minutes

Opening Moves (Introduction) (5 minutes)

- Review purpose of protocol.
- Review agreements (norms) of the team.
- Identify facilitator and participants.

Review Norms and Guidelines (5 minutes)

Norm: I agree to listen and think about you and what you are thinking in exchange for your doing the same for me.

Guidelines: Each person

- has equal time to talk.
- does not interrupt, give advice, or break in with a personal story.
- agrees that confidentiality shall be maintained.
- does not criticize or complain about others during their time to talk.

Preparation

- Facilitator asks each participant to find a partner.
- Next, the facilitator presents a prompt for each participant to share with the other (*e.g., What are you thinking about most today or this week? What do you need to discuss to be fully present for today's work? What are you looking forward to today? What are you confused by or challenged by?*).

First Cycle

- The facilitator asks the first participant to share his response with the second participant.

Second Cycle

- The facilitator calls out "switch" and asks the second participant to share her response with the first participant.

 Available for download at **us.corwin.com/rigorouspblbydesign** under the "Preview" tab

Sample Agreements Resources

Reflect on the established classroom, department, and schoolwide agreements. Do the stated agreements in the classroom, department, and school align with those shown below? Do they focus on adult and student learning? How could you infuse the following agreements into your classroom to better enable students to focus their efforts on learning?

SAMPLE AGREEMENTS

- We have a clear way to make collective decisions.
- We have a clear strategy to talk about challenges in our learning and in our group.
- We use inquiry to understand each other's ideas and intentions and to find collective solutions.
- We always check in with others to make sure they are clear on expectations and ready to learn.
- We explain our thoughts and actions to each other.
- We define important words and use learning intentions, success criteria, and examples to help everyone understand.
- We are passionate about our ideas and listen to the passionate ideas of others.

NEXT STEPS

- Inspect your current agreements and protocols to ensure they are transparent and linked to creating a community of confident learners.

- Develop a language of learning that aligns with your success criteria at the surface, deep, and transfer levels.

- Build rubrics and create a common conception of progress and growth.

- Provide pre- and postassessments to measure growth and proficiency with students.

- Use protocols to support students in discussing their growth, failures, and how they can give and receive feedback to improve.

CHAPTER 6

Reflections on PBL Practice

There was a serendipitous moment in my classroom when I witnessed my students present solutions to a panel of adults and I realized they didn't have the faintest idea what they were talking about. They had spent a significant amount of time going through the routines and rituals of project-based learning; they had built great products, engaged in rigorous group processes, and had spent quality time using materials and engaging with others to complete their project. They had "learned by doing." They learned valuable skills in working with others, how to meet deadlines, how to ensure their product looked professional, and how to present to a panel. These are valuable skills and are needed in life, but I did not specifically design for and target competency in core content and confidence in learning surface-, deep-, and transfer-level learning in a collaborative setting.

I realized that the project routines students were engaging in made for a busy classroom but not necessarily one that focused on learning. I found that often I was a manager talking about how to find certain resources, identifying how long certain activities should take, addressing conflict management, and discussing consequences for not meeting deadlines. This oriented students to focus on completion of tasks and getting things done. As Doyle (1986) found, typical teaching is about (a) creating and sustaining order in the classroom and (b) moving students through the curriculum. Project-based teaching can lead to the same typical place: (a) organizing project teams and (b) moving students through a project. In other words, regardless of the methodology, teachers and students can default to a management-style orientation, focusing on tasks, resources, and group structures and slip away from the intentional focus of learning. Take for example, the use of Critical Friends Team protocols in the PBL environment. Most of my experience with this protocol in PBL communities has been associated with the evaluation of projects (i.e., the curriculum) based on project criteria (e.g., does it have an entry event, a grouping strategy, an authentic audience, a project calendar?) rather than the impact of that project on students and how the project will enable students to progress from surface to deep to transfer learning.

After that epiphany in the classroom, I began shifting my presentations to a debate style back and forth where the adult panel questioned student logic and team solutions. Likened to ESPN's Hot Seat, students were routinely required to showcase their thinking and encounter feedback that was soft on them but hard on content. I started to see project structures (such as the entry document) as a way to home in on learning intentions and success criteria. I began using the Know/Need to Know list as a way of challenging prior knowledge and targeting workshops to specific needs using instructional strategies that were more often than not directive. I began looking for ways to capture minute-by-minute information on student performance and using formative assessment practices to improve their learning and to work with them so that they could find ways to improve their own learning. I began making a list of what teaching strategies seemed to work when students were encountering surface-level knowledge versus deep-level knowledge. I began encouraging students to note what learning strategies appeared to be helpful during their learning journey.

This was a pivotal point in my teaching—I worked to see student learning from their perspective. I needed a flashlight to shine a light on their hidden learning lives, and I needed a megaphone to amplify such information to the entire class. It was during this time that I realized that I spent too much time on teaching and not enough time on learning. I witnessed my own transformation from a project-based teacher to a teacher focused on learning who considered projects as a useful means of delivery. I had spent hours upon hours designing entry events and engaging project ideas, performance-based rubrics, group assignments, and group contracts under the wrong premise. My focus was largely on curriculum design, finding resources, searching for snazzy technology, and attempting to wow kids into loving the subject.

I somehow forgot about their learning, their thinking, and their progress. I somehow thought emotional engagement equated to cognitive engagement. I wasn't directly focused on their learning, what they thought, how they thought, and why they thought what they thought. I wasn't linking their learning to my actions. I wasn't directly focusing my actions on making a change to student learning. My actions were not actively engaging all learners and evoking responses from each student on their learning so that I, and all students, could celebrate successes and make changes to improve academic progress and proficiency. I didn't deeply inspect daily classroom routines to ensure that children were learning what they needed to be learning. Unfortunately, the data I was collecting was about the project and not the learning. I should have been focused more on making decision-driven data collection on learning.

Of course, we can have snazzy, techy, engaging projects that are emotionally engaging, but our projects and our actions must first and foremost be anchored in what makes a substantial impact on learning. We can do this through designing and implementing our projects from a place of learning and of specific actions that ensure clarity, challenge, and culture are embedded. Moreover, we can best do this when we have colleagues working with us to think through project design, implementation, and the impact of projects relative to student learning.

> Of course, we can have snazzy, techy, engaging projects that are emotionally engaging, but our projects and our actions must first and foremost be anchored in what makes a substantial impact on learning.

WORKING TOGETHER FOR IMPACT

The ultimate criterion of academic success for a teacher, department, school, or larger district system is that a substantial change in student learning of content and 21st century outcomes has occurred over an established period of time (e.g., over the course of a project or an academic year). As Graham Nuthall (2007) argues,

> Generally, effective teaching means students learn what you intend them to learn (or some part of what you intend). You may want them to acquire new knowledge and beliefs, new skills or different attitudes, or some mixture of all of these. But whatever you intend, in order to know if you have been effective, you must have some way of knowing what your students believed, knew, could do, or felt before you taught them and what your students believed, knew, could do, or felt after you taught them. Learning, of whatever kind, is about change, and unless you know what has changed in the minds, skills, and attitudes of your students, you cannot really know how effective you have been. (p. 35)

If change is the goal, teachers and learners must gather defensible and dependable evidence to determine their efficacy in learning. The three major shifts (clarity, challenge, and culture) discussed in this book have a high probability of enhancing student confidence (assessment-capable learning, growth mindset, and collaboration) and competence (surface, deep, and transfer). As a means of ensuring that such probability equates to reality, the actions of teachers must be continually tested through quality evaluation of student learning, and this is best done in a larger educational community (Dufour and Fullan, 2012).

To understand and respond to student performance in an effort to create a high yield in learning, educators (and students) should engage in reviewing student progress and proficiency together, identify what practices are standard and customizable to improve learning, and leverage PBL as a codifying instructional methodology. To review student progress and proficiency collectively, teacher or student teams should consider using the following four questions (see Figure 6.1) derived from Richard DuFour, Rebecca DuFour, Robert Eaker, and Thomas Many (2010).

FIGURE 6.1 Systemwide Professional Learning Community Priorities

QUESTIONS	SOLUTIONS
What is it we want our students to learn? What knowledge, skills, and dispositions do we expect them to acquire as a result of this course, this grade level, and this unit of instruction?	• Establish clear learning intentions and success criteria for all grade levels and disciplines
How will we know if each student is learning each of the skills, concepts, and dispositions we have deemed most essential?	• Establish rubrics to measure student progress and proficiency in relation to surface-, deep-, and transfer-level success criteria
How will we respond when some of our students do not learn? What process will we put in place to ensure students receive additional time and support for learning in a way that is timely, precise, diagnostic, directive, and systematic? How will we enrich and extend the learning for students who are already proficient?	• Align instructional-, feedback-, and learning-based strategies with surface-, deep-, and transfer-level success criteria • Collect evidence establishing that the strategies are effective over time.
How will we work collaboratively to inspect student progress and proficiency data? In light of such data, how will we respond?	• Develop and improve teacher and student teams through protocols and agreements.

SOURCE: Adapted from DuFour, DuFour, Eaker, & Many (2010).

By implementing the three design shifts laid out in this book, departments, schools, and districts will benefit from the academic boost they will provide. By establishing clear learning intentions and success criteria in every class, all students regardless of teacher, class, or school will have clarity and the benefit of a standard expectation level. Next, by developing common rubrics that align with success criteria at surface, deep, and transfer levels, all teachers and students have flexibility to have choice in assessment instrumentation, a common conception and means for measuring student performance (progress and proficiency), and the opportunity for all students to meet transfer-level expectations (rigor for all). By working toward a common instructional, feedback, and learning model, all teachers and students can reference strategies that have a high probability of impacting learning. Though this could happen with other instructional models, PBL may be the best strategy to codify these shifts. When everyone has a common language and common means for working collaboratively, a culture that focuses on learning will permeate the school and enable students and teachers to be confident and competent in their learning and teaching.

RETOOLING PBL TO SERVE AS A VEHICLE FOR CONFIDENCE AND COMPETENCE

To ensure that students are progressing at a rate of one year's growth for one year's time, the three design shifts of clarity, challenge, and culture should be strongly considered. These design shifts are not limited to the PBL methodology, however. PBL is a pedagogical vehicle that not only could integrate these shifts but could meet other 21st century outcomes, mimic work-related actions of the 21st century, and give students the opportunities to solve real-world problems in real time. The work mainly comes down to aligning actions with those strategies that make a substantial impact on student learning.

The aforementioned shifts allow us to dig deeper into an instructional approach that is strongly underpinned by surface, deep, and transfer learning and to develop learners' responsibility for their learning through the development of a growth mindset, assessment capabilities, and collaboration. This book has attempted to provide specific actions that have a high probability of yielding a high impact, provided that they are tethered to impact data. We know that there is no such thing as a "high-impact strategy" only a high-probability impact strategy.

Competency is currency in life; and there are essential understandings, knowledge, and skills that must be learned deeply and that require intervention from others (namely teachers). When students have built a foundational level of knowledge and skill and can relate and extend that understanding to authentic problems, they are on the road to being well prepared for their future. I'm a big fan of putting a big C on content knowledge. There is a need to have core knowledge to be a critical thinker, to collaborate, to communicate, and to create. Underpinning this pursuit of content, is the critical importance of confidence to self-monitor and leverage peer and adult resources, giving and receiving feedback, and seeking guidance to continually progress. Those who have confidence don't just try harder, they take the risk to try differently and do so in a public space and in a culture that leverages peer interaction and feedback; a culture that values their voice and choice. PBL is a beautiful

> PBL is a beautiful and elegant model to drive learners to meet these outcomes (along with so many other outcomes) and is in many ways a means to envelop disparate instructional methods together with an active teacher to meet substantial gains.

and elegant model to drive learners to meet these outcomes (along with so many other outcomes) and is in many ways a means to envelop disparate instructional methods together with an active teacher to meet substantial gains.

In PBL, teachers facilitate the problem-solving process and unapologetically direct learning by continually accessing and utilizing students' prior knowledge in daily practice. I encourage you to work consistently to design the learning experience so that the focus of your efforts and that of students is on the learning. In my own journey of enhancing the learning capacity of all children and adults, I have found the following shifts to be critical.

- Students need to be absolutely clear on what they are expected to learn, where they are in their learning, and what next steps they need to take to advance their learning. Their understanding of their learning and use of that learning should transcend any project situation or context.

- Students need to learn knowledge and skills thoroughly, requiring an understanding of basic to advanced knowledge to fully understand and use knowledge to make a difference in their lives and those of others. This requires different instructional interventions and modes of feedback.

- Students need to be able to talk about their learning, monitor their learning, advocate for next steps in their learning, and be a part of a culture that focuses on and models such efforts.

I sincerely hope this text was beneficial for you to implement practices that have a high probability for enhancing student learning.

Afterword

Anyone who has noticed the surging popularity of project-based learning might assume that we have entered the golden age of PBL. Glowing media accounts share compelling stories of students tackling real-world problems in PBL classrooms. To help general audiences understand this instructional approach, a feature-length documentary called *Most Likely to Succeed* (Dintersmith, 2015) takes viewers inside High Tech High in San Diego, California, for a close-up look at thoughtful teachers and engaged students tackling ambitious projects. XQ Super School, a $100 million philanthropic project, is underwriting the launch of ten high schools that aim to radically transform US education. Nearly all the winners, selected by expert judges from a pool of seven hundred proposals, incorporate some version of PBL. The Deeper Learning Network, an alliance of exemplary PBL school design organizations, continues to advance the field by hosting conferences and compiling research. The Buck Institute for Education (BIE), a nonprofit that advocates high-quality PBL as a strategy to prepare students for successful lives, is experiencing exponential growth in demand for professional development. (Full disclosure: I serve on the BIE National Faculty and contribute to BIE publications.)

Yet for all the activity, I'd argue that we're just at the start of the PBL groundswell. By my best estimates, only about one percent of US students attend schools that put projects at the center of instruction (Boss & Krauss, 2014). Beyond these wall-to-wall PBL institutions, many more schools and districts introduce project-based learning as an occasional instructional practice interspersed with more traditional teaching. A common goal is that by offering students at least some project experiences, students will acquire the blend of knowledge and skills that the National Research Council has found to be essential preparation for 21st century success. Students who develop these competencies will be able to transfer learning to solve new problems, thus preparing them for future challenges in careers and citizenship (National Research Council, 2012).

For all the promise of PBL, why isn't this approach more widespread? The simple answer is it's hard to do PBL well. Most of today's teachers did not experience this style of instruction when they were students. Only recently have preservice programs started to emphasize PBL teaching strategies.

That means teachers often have to build their PBL "muscle," and may experience growing pains as they rethink how they go about curriculum design, instruction, and assessment. Projects developed without attention to quality indicators might be fun or engaging for students, but can fall short when it comes to academic value. Poorly designed or managed projects can waste precious class time, misdirect energy, and fail to achieve learning goals (Larmer, Mergendoller, & Boss, 2015).

With this book, Michael McDowell advances an important and timely conversation about how to do PBL well. He brings an insider's perspective to project-based learning as a former teacher and instructional coach in wall-to-wall PBL schools. As he acknowledges in the introduction, he's a passionate proponent of PBL, calling it a "beautiful" way of learning that all children deserve to experience. But as he also relates, he has seen—even in his own classroom—the shortcomings of projects that emphasize "getting things done" over deep and purposeful engagement with content. He acknowledges research from John Hattie and others that points to relatively low impact of PBL on student achievement.

To improve learning outcomes of PBL, McDowell focuses squarely on the *L* in the acronym. He doesn't shy away from hard questions, namely, *How can educators design PBL to maximize student learning at surface, deep, and transfer levels? How can we help students advance their learning journeys by making sure they understand where they are heading, where they are now, which next steps are appropriate, and how they can improve their learning and that of others?* By applying research, he recommends practical moves teachers can make to increase students' confidence and competence as learners. Of course, that means more research is needed to determine the effect size of the interventions he suggests.

In many ways, McDowell delivers a tough-love message just as PBL is gaining support around the globe. I count myself among the PBL advocates who want all students to find meaning and challenge in their education. Again and again, I've seen projects ignite students' curiosity and give them a greater voice in learning. These are important outcomes if we hope to turn around alarming declines in student engagement and close the persistent achievement gap. To his credit, McDowell challenges us to make sure PBL isn't effective only sometimes or that it succeeds only with certain learners. As the PBL movement continues to grow and mature, this is advice worth heeding.

—Suzie Boss, Author of
Bringing Innovation to School and
Reinventing Project-Based Learning

APPENDIX A. Project Design Template

PROJECT DESIGN		
STEP 1: Learning Intention(s)		
STEP 2: Success Criteria		
Surface	Deep	Transfer
STEP 3: Driving Question(s)		
Context		
STEP 4: Tasks		
Surface	Deep	Transfer
STEP 5: Entry Event		
Scenario . . . Expectations . . . Patron . . . Format . . .		
WORKSHOPS		
Surface	Deep	Transfer

PROJECT CALENDAR					
	Monday	Tuesday	Wednesday	Thursday	Friday
Week 1 *[Phase 1 and Phase 2]*					
Week 2 *[Phase 2 and Phase 3]*					
Week 3 *[Phase 3 and Phase 4]*					

 Available for download at **us.corwin.com/rigorouspblbydesign** under the "Preview" tab

APPENDIX B. Sample Projects

PROJECT 1: Whose Bug Is It Anyway?

Level: Kindergarten

Subject: Science

The following project covers several interdependent Next Generation Science Standards (California) related to Ecosystems: Animals, Plants, and Their Environment in Kindergarten. In this project, kindergarteners are being asked their opinion on whether local gardeners should introduce invasive species as a means of protecting gardens from pests. Students spend a significant amount of time understanding the similarities and differences among animals, plants, and their environment as they relate to energy consumption. Students also explore human interactions with the environment and how such interactions dramatically influence local and global environments. Students have targeted surface-, deep-, and transfer-level tasks and workshops that enable them to build a solid foundation of scientific understanding. The conclusion of the project has students explore overfishing and how such human actions disrupt energy consumption. The new context focuses on the relationships of animals, plants, environments, and humans; but it also provides a new perspective on intentionally removing species from an environment rather than introducing a new species to an environment.

Key Standards

Students who demonstrate understanding can

K-LS1-1. Use observations to describe patterns of what plants and animals (including humans) need to survive. [Clarification Statement: Examples of patterns could include that animals need to take in food but plants do not, the different kinds of food needed by different types of animals, the requirement of plants to have light, and, that all living things need water.]

K-ESS2-2. Construct an argument supported by evidence for how plants and animals (including humans) can change the environment to meet their needs. [Clarification Statement: Examples of plants and animals changing their environment could include a squirrel digs in the ground to hide its food and tree roots can break concrete.]

K-ESS3-1. Use a model to represent the relationship between the needs of different plants or animals (including humans) and the places they live. [Clarification Statement: Examples of relationships could include that deer eat buds and leaves, therefore, they usually live in forested areas, and grasses need sunlight so they often grow in meadows. Plants, animals, and their surroundings make up a system.]

K-ESS3-3. Communicate solutions that will reduce the impact of humans on the land, water, air, and/or other living things in the local environment. [Clarification Statement: Examples of human impact on the land could include cutting trees to produce paper and using resources to produce bottles. Examples of solutions could include reusing paper and recycling cans and bottles.]

PHASE 1	PHASE 2	PHASE 3	PHASE 4
• Launch project. • Conduct pre/post assessment. • Go through Know/Need to Know list.	• Engage in surface workshops. • Begin completing major tasks at surface level.	• Engage in deep learning workshops. • Postassessment • Begin completing major tasks at deep level.	• Presentation • Reflection • Provide new context for students to discuss.

(Continued)

(Continued)

PROJECT DESIGN

STEP 1: Learning Intention(s)

- **Learning Intention (1):** I can tell others why plants and animals change their environment to survive.
- **Learning Intention (2):** I can show others why plants and animals live in different environments.
- **Learning Intention (3):** I can tell others how humans can improve the local environment, which they sometimes hurt.

STEP 2: Success Criteria

Surface	Deep	Transfer
• Define *plant*, *animal*, and *environment*. • List examples of human impact.	• Relate animals and plants to their needs (e.g., energy needs). • Relate animals and plants to different environments. • Relate human impacts to animals and plants.	• Design a solution to a human-caused issue that will improve the local and global environment.

STEP 3: Driving Question(s)

How do humans improve their local and global environment to prevent the loss of animals and plants? [in your neighbor's garden]?

Context

- Invasive species (in our gardens)–insects, plants–bamboo
- Overfishing
- Plastic bottles
- Litter
- Reintroduction of a species
- Global warming

STEP 4: Tasks

Surface	Deep	Transfer
• Label key images.	• Design a visual diagram that illustrates the relationships among plants, animals, and humans.	• Select one of these problems, then present a solution to adults using text and visuals.

STEP 5: Entry Event

Scenario . . . Local gardeners want to use insects to control pests.

Expectations. . . . Present a solution that includes reasons for finding native solutions to biocontrol issues.

Patrons. . . . Local gardeners (parents, community members, staff)

Format . . . Public presentation to adults (with accompanying resources–visuals)

WORKSHOPS

Surface	Deep	Transfer
• Classification of animals, plants, and environments (four workshops reviewing animals, plants, and environments) using a jigsaw method • Read fiction and nonfiction selections on gardens.	• Draw relationships between animals and plants using nonlinguistic representation (Students will have multiple images that they must categorize to demonstrate relationships.) • Perspective analysis on human involvement with the local and global environment.	• Compare and contrast problems between overfishing (orange roughy) and our local garden.

(Continued)

(Continued)

PROJECT CALENDAR

	Monday	Tuesday	Wednesday	Thursday	Friday
Week 1 *[Phase 1 and Phase 2]*	Project launch (Local gardeners discuss biocontrol issue; include key "breadcrumbs.") Start with aphids and ladybugs. Preassessment (oral assessment) Students go through a Know/Need to Know process.	Surface workshops (How do we classify animals, plants, and environments?)	Surface Animals Reading workshop—nonfiction	Surface Plants Reading workshop—fiction	Surface Environment
Week 2 *[Phase 2 and Phase 3]*	Review Know/Need to Know list. Meet with local gardeners to discuss how plants and animals intersect in the garden. Watch a video clip on animals and plants in other environments.	Deeper workshop Relationships. Nonlinguistic representation workshop	Deeper workshops Visit the garden. Take observations and then check on categorization from previous workshop.	Deeper workshop Perspective analysis	Reading workshop—nonfiction
Week 3 *[Phase 3 and Phase 4]*	Postassessment review Know/Need to Know list	Prepare for presentations. Critical Friends Team review	Present bio control solutions to local gardeners.	Transfer workshop How do we address overfishing (orange roughy)? How is this problem similar to our garden problem? How does it differ?	Reflections

Available for download at **us.corwin.com/rigorouspblbydesign** under the "Preview" tab

PROJECT 2: Ratios, Rates, and Real Estate Oh My. . . .

Level: Sixth Grade

Subject: Mathematics

This project focuses on understanding and applying unit rates (comparing a quantity to one unit of another quantity) to common practices in society. Students are expected to understand rates (ratios of two quantities with different units) and how to calculate rates (e.g., unit pricing and constant speed). This project requires students to use their knowledge and application of rates in the world of real estate and specifically how absorption rates (i.e., dividing the number of sales by number of available homes) impact various communities by influencing short-term and long-term appraisals. The project concludes with a one-day problem on applying the same math content in a different context. For instance, the project asks student to identify the absorption rates of different brands of paper towels and how such information may impact consumer decision making.

Key Standards

CCSS.MATH.CONTENT.6.RP.A.1

Understand the concept of a ratio and use ratio language to describe a ratio relationship between two quantities.

CCSS.MATH.CONTENT.6.RP.A.2

Understand the concept of a unit rate a/b associated with a ratio a:b with b ≠ 0, and use rate language in the context of a ratio relationship.

CCSS.MATH.CONTENT.6.RP.A.3

Use tables of equivalent ratios, tape diagrams, double number line diagrams, or equations.

MATHEMATICAL PRACTICES

All Mathematical Practices are covered.

PHASE 1	PHASE 2	PHASE 3	PHASE 4
• Launch project. • Conduct pre/postassessment. • Go through Know/Need to Know list.	• Engage in surface workshops. • Begin completing major tasks at surface level.	• Engage in deep-learning workshops. • Postassessment • Begin completing major tasks at deep level.	• Presentation • Reflection • Provide new context for students to discuss.

(Continued)

(Continued)

PROJECT DESIGN

STEP 1: Learning Intention(s)

- I can use rates and unit rates to solve problems.
- I can express rates and unit rates to solve problems using models, tables, and line drawings.

STEP 2: Success Criteria

Surface	Deep	Transfer
• Define *rate, unit rate, unit pricing, ratio, constant speed, average speed.* • Solve unit rate problems using one method. • Describe unit rate problems using a visual representation.	• Relate rate terms. • Solve unit rate problems using different methods (multiplication expression or division expression). • Relate models, tables, and line drawings to unit rate problems.	• Apply models, tables, and line drawings to various contexts in which rates and unit rates are germane.

STEP 3: Driving Question(s)

How do rates enable people to make decisions (such as housing appraisals in your local community)?

Context

- Absorption rates (e.g., paper towels, real estate)
- Heart rate (monitoring)

STEP 4: Tasks

Surface	Deep	Transfer
• Complete a number talk expressing different ways to find ratios. • Present to others how ratios compare two quantities that have the same unit. • Solve rate problems numerically and verbally.	• Compare and contrast different ways (models) to represent rates. • Show processes and solutions to rate problems using different methods to represent data.	• Present multiple representations of rates to an audience to help inform decision making.

STEP 5: Entry Event

Scenario . . . Local community real estate

Expectations . . . Use multiple representations of rates to influence decision making.

Patron . . . Home buyers, sellers, and real estate agents

Format . . . Presentation from real estate agent—Preview online Huffington Post article "What Is Absorption Rate in Real Estate and Why Is It Important?"

WORKSHOPS

Surface	Deep	Transfer
• Direct instruction workshop: What is a rate? How is it calculated? How can one convey a rate?	• Provide direct modeling of a rate problem using multiple methods of representation. Students practice in triads to solve a rate problem and demonstrate the solution using different representations. Present representations to the larger class using academic vocabulary.	• Critical Friends Team feedback on real estate models • Compare and contrast absorption of paper towels with absorption of real estate.

(Continued)

(Continued)

PROJECT CALENDAR

	Monday	Tuesday	Wednesday	Thursday	Friday
Week 1 [Phase 1 and Phase 2]	Project launch preassessment	Surface workshops What are rates?	Surface Rate calculations Different interpretations	Practice/feedback	Review Know/ Need to Know list. Surface workshops Practice Feedback
Week 2 [Phase 2 and Phase 3]	Deeper workshop Relationships Modeling practice	Deeper workshop Relationships Modeling practice	Deeper workshop Relationships Modeling practice	Deeper workshop Relationships Modeling practice	Postassessment review Know/Need to Know list
Week 3 [Phase 3 and Phase 4]	Review real estate problem.	Transfer workshop— Reviewing models. Critical Friends Team review with others.	Present to local community.	Transfer workshop Transfer understanding of learned concept (i.e., rate) to a new context.	Reflections

 Available for download at **us.corwin.com/rigorouspblbydesign** under the "Preview" tab

158

PROJECT 3: Changing or Maintaining Our Imperialist Imperative

Level: High School

Subject: Social Studies and English Language Arts

The following project focuses students on understanding the significant impact of industrialized nations on developing nations. Specifically, the project addresses parts of History-Social Sciences Content Standard 10.4:

Key Standards

> **10.4.1 Describe the rise of industrial economies and their link to imperialism and colonialism (e.g., the role played by national security and strategic advantage; moral issues raised by the search for national hegemony, Social Darwinism, and the missionary impulse; material issues such as land, resources, and technology).**
>
> **10.4.2 Discuss the locations of the colonial rule of such nations as England, France, Germany, Italy, Japan, the Netherlands, Russia, Spain, Portugal, and the United States.**
>
> **10.4.3 Explain imperialism from the perspective of the colonizers and the colonized and the varied immediate and long-term responses by the people under colonial rule.** (http://www.cde.ca.gov/be/st/ss/documents/histsocscistnd.pdf)

The project focuses on military, social, and economic reasons for industrialized nations to interact and fundamentally influence other nations—and on the positive and negative impacts those relationships have on both parties. The project offers students the opportunity to look at contemporary issues. First, students are faced with understanding the role of the United States in the development of and maintenance of ISIS and how to face growing local and global concerns of such a development. Students develop a thorough understanding of imperialism by looking at historical patterns and analyzing causes, characteristics, and effects of European imperialism and how such patterns reflect contemporary behavior. At the conclusion of the project, students look at emerging countries and their spread of imperialism to other nations (e.g., China on Taiwan) and what role the United States should play in an omnipresent global community.

PHASE 1	PHASE 2	PHASE 3	PHASE 4
• Launch project. • Conduct pre/postassessment. • Go through Know/Need to Know list.	• Engage in surface workshops. • Begin completing major tasks at surface level.	• Engage in deep-learning workshops. • Postassessment • Begin completing major tasks at deep level.	• Presentation • Reflection • Provide new context for students to discuss.

(Continued)

PROJECT DESIGN

STEP 1: Learning Intention(s)

The Industrialized nations' desire for abundant resources and new markets for their goods coupled with feelings of cultural superiority (such as Social Darwinism) and increased military power allowed for and encouraged imperial expansion. Imperialism had lasting positive and negative effects.

STEP 2: Success Criteria

Surface	Deep	Transfer
• The student lists political, economic, and social reasons that drove 19th century European imperialism.	• The student relates the causes, characteristics, and effects of 19th century European imperialism, making evaluations of specific countries' imperialistic actions.	• The student evaluates the present day legacy of imperialism in at least one region of the world. • The student makes a hypothesis on the impact imperialism has in various contemporary contexts.

STEP 3: Driving Question(s)

How do the United States and other industrialized imperial nations prevent creating new global enemies?

Context

- ISIS
- Global trade
- Economic sanctions

STEP 4: Tasks

Surface	Deep	Transfer
Address the following in pairs and with the class: • Identify conditions of imperialism. • Define terms and concepts of *Social Darwinism, patriarchy,* and *capitalism.* • Identify types and sources of power: political, economic, religious, ideological	Using case study material for 19th century US, European, Middle Eastern, African, and Asian nations, build a graphic organizer that • identifies which nations had power and what type. • identifies the basis for the types of powers listed above. • explains how that power was exercised. • determines what impact imperialistic nations had on each nation. • identifies the conditions that existed in each nation that either resulted in it becoming a dominant or dominated nation.	• Develop a white paper on the best solution for the United States and allied forces to employ to ensure the safety and security of the people around the world by defeating groups such as ISIS. • Present three actions the United States and allied nations can take to mitigate risk to citizens while building positive relations with previously imperialized regions of the world.

STEP 5: Entry Event

Scenario . . . Expansion of ISIS is causing the US government to rethink its military strategy.

Expectations . . . Present three actions to a panel on what actions the United States can take to mitigate risk to citizens and establish positive relations in the region.

Patron . . . Social studies department

Format . . . Written memo

(Continued)

(Continued)

WORKSHOPS

Surface	Deep	Transfer
• Making sense of resources: What conditions led to imperialism?	• Ideological conflicts: Why do different people have different ideas about government, economics, and religion? • What were the causes and effects of imperial conflicts such as the Boer War, Opium War, and Raj rebellions?	• Comparative conflicts • Students will select a current world conflict and analyze the economic, political and ideological conditions that led to these conflicts and determine if they are remnants of the imperialist era practices. • Students will make predictions about current geopolitical situations and determine if the conditions are ripe for conflict and if so, what measures can be taken to avoid conflict and bring about peace and stability.

PROJECT CALENDAR

	Monday	Tuesday	Wednesday	Thursday	Friday
Week 1 *[Phase 1 and Phase 2]*	Project launch Preassessment	Surface workshop(s) (Define terms)	Surface workshop(s) (Sources and conditions)	Pair discussions/Jigsaw (Sources and conditions)	Pair discussions/Jigsaw (Sources and conditions)
Week 2 *[Phase 2 and Phase 3]*	Deep workshops(s) Ideological conflict Case study review Provide graphic organizer draft.	Deep workshop Conflict snapshot Case study review Construct graphic organizer.	Deep workshop Conflict snapshot Case study review Feedback on graphic organizer.	Deep workshop Review US actions. Complete graphic organizer.	Deep workshop Review white paper exemplars.
Week 3 *[Phase 3 and Phase 4]*	Transfer workshops Current issues Current solutions Assessment Brainstorm	Transfer workshops Current issues (looking at different contexts) Develop white paper.	Transfer workshops Critical Friends on white paper Prepare 5-minute presentation.	Present solution. Submit paper. Discuss new topics.	Reflect

PROJECT 4: Fables, Futures, and Forecasts

Level: Third Grade

Subject: English Language Arts

The following project requires students in the third grade to develop their skills in writing by developing an opinion piece that includes a point of view with a clear rationale. To receive full marks on the final product, the students must convey their ideas clearly and must provide thorough and accurate evidence that supports their opinion. To be effective, the implementation of the project must specifically focus on the targeted skill sets while using students' knowledge gained in previous years to ensure that they are concentrating on learning new writing techniques rather than focusing on the unfamiliar context. In the second grade, students spent significant time recounting stories including fables and folktales from diverse cultures and spent time determining their central message, lessons, or morals. This project relies on the students' background knowledge of this genre of literature.

The conclusion of the project has students conduct an author's speak where students present their writing to a group of parents, community members, teachers, and peers. The presentation includes a series of questions and answers in which the students must discuss how they conducted their research and reached a point of view. After the presentations, the teacher tasks students with writing a brief opinion piece on other subjects of interest that are linked to the students' prior knowledge.

Key Standards

Students who demonstrate understanding can

CCSS.ELA-LITERACY.W.3.1

Write opinion pieces on topics or texts, supporting a point of view with reasons.

CCSS.ELA-LITERACY.W.3.1.A

Introduce the topic or text they are writing about, state an opinion, and create an organizational structure that lists reasons.

CCSS.ELA-LITERACY.W.3.1.B

Provide reasons that support the opinion.

CCSS.ELA-LITERACY.W.3.1.C

Use linking words and phrases (e.g., *because, therefore, since, for example*) to connect opinion and reasons.

(Continued)

(Continued)

CCSS.ELA-LITERACY.W.3.1.D

Provide a concluding statement or section.

CCSS.ELA-LITERACY.W.3.2

Write informative/explanatory texts to examine a topic and convey ideas and information clearly.

CCSS.ELA-LITERACY.W.3.2.A

Introduce a topic and group-related information together; include illustrations when useful to aiding comprehension.

CCSS.ELA-LITERACY.W.3.2.B

Develop the topic with facts, definitions, and details.

CCSS.ELA-LITERACY.W.3.2.C

Use linking words and phrases (e.g., *also, another, and, more, but*) to connect ideas within categories of information.

CCSS.ELA-LITERACY.W.3.2.D

Provide a concluding statement or section.

PHASE 1	PHASE 2	PHASE 3	PHASE 4
• Launch project. • Conduct pre/postassessment. • Go through Know/Need to Know list.	• Engage in surface workshops. • Begin completing major tasks at surface level.	• Engage in deep-learning workshops. • Postassessment • Begin completing major tasks at deep level.	• Presentation • Reflection • Provide new context for students to discuss.

PROJECT DESIGN

STEP 1: Learning Intention(s)

- **Learning Intention (1):** I can write and support my opinion on a topic.
- **Learning Intention (2):** I can write on a topic that conveys information clearly.

STEP 2: Success Criteria

Surface	Deep	Transfer
• Use *because, therefore, since, for example.* • Identify reasons, opinions, points of view in texts and own writing.	• Link *because, therefore, since,* and *for example* to opinions and reasons. • Sequence reasons, opinion, and points of view in own writing and in text. • Connect facts, definitions, and details to backup opinion.	• Write an opinion piece that includes a clear rationale with details, definitions, and facts to enable others to understand your ideas.

STEP 3: Driving Question(s)

How do we use the lessons conveyed in the stories of our youth to [develop classroom rules]?

Context

- Classroom rules
- Study habits
- Understanding others
- Developing friendships
- Future goals and actions
- Predict our future based on our decisions

(Continued)

(Continued)

STEP 4: Tasks

Surface	Deep	Transfer
• Identify connecting words in texts. • In dyads, practice sharing and backing up opinions with facts.	• Write a series of paragraphs that sequence reasons, opinions, and points of view. • Develop a narrative organizer that relates details to specific opinions. • Review texts for connecting words, points of view, and related rationale.	• Develop an opinion piece.

STEP 5: Entry Event

Context . . . Third-grade classroom
Expectations. . . . Develop an opinion piece
Patron. . . . School community
Format. . . . Written piece and public presentation including a Q&A

WORKSHOPS

Surface	Deep	Transfer
• Workshop exploring connectors (Use *because, therefore, since, for example*.) • Identify reasons, opinions, points of view in texts and own writing.	• Review and evaluate student work in light of success criteria. • Craft organizers to link opinions to data that supports and or refutes ideas.	• Analyze the structure of an opinion piece in different situations.

	Monday	Tuesday	Wednesday	Thursday	Friday
Week 1 [Phase 1 and Phase 2]	Project launch Review fables. Review exemplar opinion pieces. Discuss success criteria. Review examples of excellence.	Surface workshops Practice writing. Dyad practice Find a fable.	Surface Identify reasons, opinions, points of view in texts and own writing. Practice writing.	Surface Practice writing.	Deep Review and evaluate student work in light of success criteria.
Week 2 [Phase 2 and Phase 3]	Practice writing.	Deeper workshops Craft organizers to link opinions to data that supports or refutes ideas.	Practice writing.	Submit draft. Receive feedback (make changes).	Deep to transfer workshops Analyze the structure of an opinion piece.
Week 3 [Phase 3 and Phase 4]	Submit draft II. Receive feedback (make changes).	Author's Speak— Based on feedback, make corrections.	Transfer workshop Craft an opinion piece developing effective study habits and review with peers using success criteria.	Reflections Analyze the structure of an opinion piece in different situations.	

Available for download at **us.corwin.com/rigorouspblbydesign** under the "Preview" tab

APPENDIX C. PBL Design Shift and Key Elements Checklist

Projects that have a high probability of making a substantial impact on student learning involve three key design shifts and, as such, possess the following elements:

CLARITY

Clear Learning Intentions   ☐

- Students have a clear understanding of what they are expected to know and be able to do.

Success Criteria   ☐

- Students have a clear understanding of surface-, deep-, and transfer-level expectations to meet established learning outcomes throughout the project phases (Phase 1 through Phase 4).

- Success criteria are void of project contexts and do not include task-specific requirements.

Task Arrangement   ☐

- Students have tasks that are aligned with surface-, deep-, and transfer-level expectations. Tasks are rich in reading, writing, and talking.

CHALLENGE

Instructional Alignment   ☐

- Instructional interventions (strategies used by teachers) are aligned with surface-, deep-, and transfer-level success criteria and tasks.

Inquiry Alignment   ☐

- Students routinely encounter activities that enable them to answer the following four questions: *Where am I going? Where am I now? What are my next steps? How do I improve my learning and that of others?*

- Teachers continually identify student progress and proficiency in relation to learning intentions and success criteria and provide feedback and instructional support that corresponds to students' level of understanding.

CULTURE

Protocols and Agreements   ☐

- Students encounter routines and norms in the classroom that allow them to have voice in describing their level of progress and proficiency (surface, deep, and transfer outcomes) and articulate when they are stuck in their learning.

- Students have choice in ways to monitor their progress, showcase their performance, and give, receive, and use feedback to move learning forward.

- Teachers and students inspect their efficacy by reviewing performance data with others.

 Available for download at **us.corwin.com/rigorouspblbydesign** under the "Preview" tab

APPENDIX D. Recommended Texts for PBL Implementation

For those interested in scaling the three key design shifts, I recommend the following:

- *Schooling by Design: Mission, Action, and Achievement* by Jay McTighe and Grant Wiggins (2007). Alexandria, VA: ASCD.

- *The Leader's Guide to 21st Century Education: 7 Steps for Schools and Districts* by Ken Kay and Valerie Greenhill (2012). Boston, MA: Pearson Education.

- *Leading With Focus: Elevating the Essentials for School and District Improvement* by Mike Schmoker (2016). Alexandria, VA: ASCD.

Glossary

Cognitive tension (also known as cognitive dissonance, cognitive discrepancy, or cognitive gap): A misalignment between what has been previously understood and what is being presented or taught.

Context: The situation or background that students encounter in a project.

Critical Friends Team: A group of teachers who strategically and routinely work together to improve student proficiency and progress levels. Teams specifically focus their efforts on reviewing student performance data and determining from such evidence successes, challenges, and next steps in teaching that will enhance student progress and proficiency. Teacher teams use structured protocols, agreements or norms, dialogue, and internal and external professional development to improve their collective learning and development.

Decontextualized learning objective: Academic goals that are not intertwined or integrated with the context of the project.

Deep learning (combining or linking ideas and skills): A level of academic complexity that requires students to relate ideas and skills to develop a comprehensive understanding of relationships and general rules or principles within a discipline.

Dessert PBL: Where teachers focus sharply on the content and skill building first, and then apply those skills to the project. (*See also* Main course PBL.)

Driving question: A question presented at the beginning of a project to orient students to learning intentions and project contexts.

Effect size: A common measure to determine the magnitude of change in student progress over time or the degree to which a variable (such as homework) impacts student achievement. The method allows researchers and practitioners to compare results on different measures, across various groups, over time, and across different scoring schemes. For interventions in education to be considered valuable, student progress and the magnitude of a variable on student achievement should have an effect size of at least 0.40. A gain of 0.40 is considered an average gain, or hinge-point to identify what is (at or above 0.40) and what is not effective (below 0.40).

Entry event: A project description that illuminates the learning intentions, success criteria, driving question, context of the problem, and the task expectations to students. The entry event also describes the person or persons (patron) seeking an answer to the driving question.

Formative assessment: A planned process in which assessment-elicited evidence of students' status is used by teachers to adjust ongoing instruction. Part of the formative assessment process is students using feedback and performance data to adjust their own learning strategies.

Formative teaching: A planned process in which teachers use a set of questions to elicit students' performance level and, in light of that evidence, make instructional decisions to enhance student learning.

Learning intentions: Brief statements that explicitly describe what students should know (i.e., content) and be able to do (i.e., skill). These brief statements anchor all other steps in project design and serve as the focal point or "end in mind" for teachers and students to continually refer to during projects.

Learning Challenge: A metaphor for the learning process which includes a learning pit, when the learner is struggling with understanding ideas and skills that are in direct conflict with her prior knowledge or current beliefs.

Main course PBL: The main course approach involves beginning a unit using PBL and teaching content and skills within the project. (*See also* Dessert PBL.)

Phase 1: Project launch: Students are introduced to the transfer-level learning expectations of the project. Students are assessed on their level of understanding of surface-, deep-, and transfer-level competence.

Phase 2: Surface workshops: Students learn surface-level information, complete surface-level tasks, and receive instruction that is at the surface level.

Phase 3: Deeper workshops: Students learn deeper-level information, complete deeper-level tasks, and receive instruction that is at the deeper level.

Phase 4: Presentations/reflections: Students present their understanding of surface- and deep-level outcomes and solve transfer-level outcomes. Students also reflect on their learning.

Professional learning community (PLC): A PLC may be defined as an ongoing process in which educators work collaboratively in recurring cycles of collective inquiry to review and respond to student achievement data in order to achieve better results for the students they serve.

Proficiency matrix: A means for analyzing proficiency and progress of student learning.

Proficiency range: The span of scores that meet the level of success on achieving surface-, deep-, and transfer-level understanding.

Project-based learning (PBL): A series of complex tasks that include planning and design, problem solving, decision making, creating artifacts, and communicating results.

Rubric: A common tool that enables teachers to assess student performance relative to progression levels of knowledge and skill along a common scale.

Scaffolding: Support teachers provide to students in attaining surface-, deep-, and transfer-level success criteria in order to meet established learning intentions. A teacher may provide many forms of scaffolding including instructional, feedback, and learning-strategy approaches. A teacher typically develops a range of workshops to scaffold learning across the natural learning progression of surface, deep, and transfer learning.

Success criteria: Success criteria specify what students must demonstrate at the surface, deep, and transfer levels to meet learning intentions.

Surface learning: A level of academic complexity that requires students to understand single and multiple ideas or skills.

Transfer learning (extending ideas and skills): A level of academic complexity that requires students to apply deeper-level understanding and skills within and across various disciplines and contexts.

Workshop: A term typically used in PBL to describe a lesson embedded within a project. Workshops are developed for each learning intention across the progression levels and then are sequenced from surface to deeper levels of learning.

References

Albanese, M. A., & Mitchell, S. (1993). Problem-based learning: A review of literature on its outcomes and implementation issues. *Academic Medicine, 68*(1), 52–81.

Argyris, C., & Schön, D. (1974). *Theory in practice: Increasing professional effectiveness.* San Francisco, CA: Jossey-Bass.

Ausubel, D. P. (1968). *Educational psychology: A cognitive view.* New York, NY: Holt, Rinehart & Winston.

Barton, P. E. (2006). *"Failing" schools, "succeeding" schools: How can you tell?* Washington, DC: American Federation of Teachers.

Bersin, J. (2014, March 15). *Why companies fail to engage today's workforce: The overwhelmed employee.* Retrieved from http://www.forbes.com/sites/joshbersin /2014/03/15/why-companies-fail-to-engage-todays-workforce-the-overwhelmed-employee/#49f9362e2b94

Boss, S., & Krauss, J. (2014). *Reinventing project-based learning: Your field guide to real-world projects in the digital age* (2nd ed.). Eugene, OR: International Society for Technology in Education.

Briceño, E. (2015, November 15). Growth mindset: Clearing up some common confusions. *KQED Mindshift.* Retrieved from http://ww2.kqed.org/mindshift /2015/11/16/growth-mindset-clearing-up-some-common-confusions/

Brooks, J. G., & Brooks, M. G. (1993). *In search of understanding: The case for constructivist classrooms.* Alexandria, VA: ASCD.

Christensen, C. M., & Shu, K. (2006). *What is an organization's culture?* (Rev.; Harvard Business School Background Note 399-104). Cambridge, MA: Harvard Business School.

Clarke, S. (2008) *Active learning through formative assessment.* Philadelphia, PA: Trans-Atlantic.

Clarke, S. (2015) *Outstanding formative assessment: Culture and practice.* Philadelphia, PA: Trans-Atlantic.

Dagyar, M., & Demirel, M. (2015). Effects of problem-based learning on academic achievement: A meta-analysis study. *Education and Science, 40*(181), 139–174.

Dintersmith, T. (Producer), & Whiteley, G. (Director). (2015). *Most likely to succeed* [Motion picture]. US: One Potato Productions.

Dochy, F., Segers, M., Van den Bossche, P., & Gijbels, D. (2003). Effects of problem-based learning: A meta-analysis. *Learning and Instruction, 13*(5), 533–568.

Doyle, W. (1986). Classroom organization and management. In M. C. Wittrock (Ed.), *Handbook of research on teaching* (3rd ed., pp. 392–431). New York: Macmillan.

Driscoll, M. P. (1994). *Psychology of learning for instruction.* Boston, MA: Allyn & Bacon.

Duffy, T. M., & Jonassen, D. H. (1991). Constructivism: New implications for instructional technology? *Educational Technology, 31*(3), 7–12.

DuFour, R., DuFour, R., Eaker, R., & Many, T. (2010). *Learning by doing: A handbook for professional learning at work.* Bloomington, IN: Solution Tree.

DuFour, R., & Fullan, M. (2012). *Cultures built to last: Systemic PLCs at work.* Bloomington, IN: Solution Tree.

DuFour, R., & Marzano, R. (2011). *Leaders of learning: How district, school, and classroom leaders improve student achievement.* Bloomington, IN: Solution Tree.

Dumont, H., Istance, D., & Benavides, F. (2010). *The nature of learning: Using research to inspire practice.* Retrieved from http://www.oecd.org/edu/ceri/50300814.pdf

Dweck, C. S. (2007). *Mindset: The new psychology of success.* New York, NY: Ballantine Books.

Dweck, C. S. (2015, September 22). Carol Dweck revisits the 'growth mindset.' *Education Week, 35*(5), 20, 24. Retrieved from http://www.edweek.org/ew/articles/2015/09/23/carol-dweck-revisits-the-growth-mindset.html

Gijbels, D., Dochy, F., Van den Bossche, P., & Segers, M. (2005). Effects of problem-based learning: A meta-analysis from the angle of assessment. *Review of Educational Research, 75*(1), 27–61.

Gilhooly, K. J. (1990). Cognitive psychology and medical diagnosis. *Applied Cognitive Psychology, 4*(4), 261–272.

Haas, M. (2005). Teaching methods for secondary algebra: A meta-analysis of findings. *NASSP Bulletin, 89*(642), 24–46.

Haberman, M. (1991). The pedagogy of poverty versus good teaching. *Phi Delta Kappan, 73*(4), 290–294.

Hallermann, S., Larmer, J., & Mergendoller, J. R. (2014). *PBL in the elementary grades: Step-by-step guidance, tools and tips for standards-focused K–5 projects.* Novato, CA: Buck Institute of Education.

Harvey, T. R., Bearley, W. L., & Corkrum, S. M. (1997). *The practical decision maker: A handbook for decision making and problem solving in organizations.* Lanham, MD: R&L Education.

Hattie, J. (2009). *Visible learning: A synthesis of over 800 meta-analyses relating to achievement.* New York, NY: Routledge.

Hattie, J. (2011). *Visible learning: Maximizing impact on learning for teachers.* New York, NY: Routledge.

Hattie, J. (2012). *Visible learning for teachers: Maximizing impact on learning.* New York: Routledge.

Hattie, J., & Donoghue, G. (2016). Learning strategies: A synthesis and conceptual model. *npj Science of Learning, 1.* doi:10.1038/npjscilearn.2016.13

Hattie, J., & Timperley, H. (2007). The power of feedback. *Review of Educational Research, 77*(1), 81–112. Retrieved from http://education.qld.gov.au/staff/development/performance/resources/readings/power-feedback.pdf

Hook, P., & Cassé, B. (2013). *Solo taxonomy in the early years: Making connections for belonging, being and becoming.* Invercargill, New Zealand: Essential Resources Educational.

Larmer, J., & Mergendoller, J. R. (2010a). *The main course, not dessert: How are students reaching 21st century goals? With 21st century project based learning.* Novato, CA: Buck Institute for Education.

Larmer, J., & Mergendoller, J. R. (2010b). Seven essentials for project-based learning. *Educational Leadership, 68*(1), 34–37. Retrieved from http://www.ascd.org/publications/educational_leadership/sept10/vol68/num01/Seven_Essentials_for_Project-Based_Learning.aspx

Larmer, J., & Mergendoller, J. R. (2015, April 21) [Web log post]. *Gold standard PBL: Essential project design elements.* Retrieved from http://bie.org/blog/gold_standard_pbl_essential_project_design_elements

Larmer, J., Mergendoller, J. R., & Boss, S. (2015). *Setting the standard for project based learning: A proven approach to rigorous classroom instruction.* Alexandria, VA: ASCD.

Larson, A. (2016, August 23). *Balancing approaches for PBL success* [Web log post]. Retrieved from http://www.bie.org/blog/balancing_approaches_for_pbl_success

Lavery, L. (2008). *Self-regulated learning for academic success: An evaluation of instructional techniques* (Doctoral dissertation). University of Auckland, New Zealand.

Leary, H., Walker, A., Shelton, B. E., & Fitt, M. H. (2013). Exploring the relationships between tutor background, tutor training, and student learning: A problem-based learning meta-analysis. *Interdisciplinary Journal of Problem-based Learning, 7*(1), 6.

Lencioni, P. (2014). *Three signs of a miserable job: A fable for managers (and their employees).* New York, NY: Wiley.

Lencioni, P. (2015). *The truth about employee engagement: A fable about addressing the three root causes of job misery.* San Francisco, CA: Jossey-Bass.

Markham, T., Larmer, J., & Ravitz, J. (2003). *Project based learning: A guide to standards-focused project based learning for middle and high school teachers* (2nd Rev. ed). Novato, CA: Buck Institute of Education.

Marshall, H. E., & Skelton, J. R. (1908). *Stories of Beowulf.* London, England: Thomas Nelson and Sons.

Marzano, R. (2007). *The art and science of teaching: A comprehensive framework for effective instruction.* Alexandria, VA: ASCD.

Marzano, R. (2009). *Standards-based reporting and formative assessment: On the road to a highly reliable organization* [DVD]. Bloomington, IN: Solution Tree.

Marzano, R. (with Pickering, D. J, Heflebower, T., Boogren, T., & Kanold-McIntyre, J.). (2012). *Becoming a reflective teacher.* Bloomington, IN: Solution Tree.

Marzano, R., & Waters, T. (2009). *District leadership that works: Striking the right balance.* Bloomington, IN: Solution Tree.

McDowell, M. (2009). *Group leadership in the project-based learning classroom* (Doctoral dissertation). Retrieved from ProQuest. (3370197)

McDowell, M. (2013, January 3). *Putting the know in need to know.* [Web log post]. Retrieved from https://edmovers.wordpress.com/?s=know+list

McLean Davies, L., Anderson, M., Deans, J., Dinham, S., Griffin, P., Kameniar, B., . . . & Tyler, D. (2013). Masterly preparation: Embedding clinical practice in a graduate pre-service teacher education programme. *Journal of Education for Teaching International Research and Pedagogy, 39*(1), 93–106.

McTighe, J., & Wiggins, G. (2013). *Essential questions: Opening doors to student understanding.* Alexandria, VA: ASCD.

Mergendoller, J. R., Markham, T., Ravitz, J., & Larmer, J. (2006). Pervasive management of project based learning: Teachers as guides and facilitators. In C. M. Everson & C. S. Weinstein (Eds.), *Handbook of classroom management: Research, practice, and contemporary issues* (pp. 583–615), Mahwah, NJ: Erlbaum.

Mergendoller, J. R., & Thomas, J. W. (2005). *Managing project-based learning: Principles from the field.* Retrieved from http://www.bie.org/tmp/research/research managePBL.pdf

Muller, D. A. (2008). *Designing effective multimedia for physics education* (Doctoral dissertation). Retrieved from http://www.physics.usyd.edu.au/super/theses/PhD(Muller).pdf

National Research Council. (2012). *Education for life and work: Developing transferable knowledge and skills in the 21st century.* Washington, DC: The National Academies Press. Retrieved from https://www.nap.edu/read/13398/chapter/1

Newman, M. J. (2005). Problem based learning: An introduction and overview of the key features of the approach. *Journal of Veterinary Medical Education, 32*(1), 12–20.

Nottingham, J. (2010). *Challenging learning: Theory, effective, practice, and lesson ideas to create optimal learning conditions for learning with pupils aged 5 to 18.* Cramlington, England: JN Publishing.

Nuthall, G. A. (2001, December). *The cultural myths and the realities of teaching and learning.* Unpublished Jean Herbison Lecture, 2001. Retrieved from http://www.educationalleaders.govt.nz/Pedagogy-and-assessment/Evidence-based-leadership/Data-gathering-and-analysis/The-cultural-myths-and-realities-of-teaching-and-learning

Nuthall, G. A. (2005, May). The cultural myths and the realities of teaching and learning: A personal journey. *Teachers College Record, 107*(5), 895–934.

Nuthall, G. A. (2007). *The hidden lives of learners.* Wellington: New Zealand Council for Educational Research.

Ochoa, T. A., Gerber, M. M., Leafstedt, J. M., Hough, S., Kyle, S., Rogers-Adkinson, D., & Kumar, P. (2001). Web technology as a teaching tool: A multicultural special education case. *Educational Technology & Society, 4*(1), 50–60.

Ochoa, T. A., & Robinson, J. M. (2005). Revisiting group consensus: Collaborative learning dynamic during a problem-based activity in education. *Teacher Education and Special Education, 28*(1). Retrieved from http://files.eric.ed.gov/fulltext/EJ696157.pdf

Perkins, D. (2014). *Future wise: Educating our children for a changing world.* San Francisco, CA: Jossey-Bass.

Pink, D. H. (2011). *Drive: The surprising truth about what motivates us.* New York, NY: Riverhead Books.

Popham, W. J. (2011). *Classroom assessment: What teachers need to know* (6th ed.). Boston, MA: Pearson Education.

Popham, W. J. (2013). Waving the flag for formative assessment. *Educational Week.* Retrieved from http://www.edweek.org/ew/articles/2013/01/09/15popham.h32.html

Reeves, D. B. (2009). *Leading change in your school: How to conquer myths, build commitment, and get results.* Alexandria, VA: ASCD.

Rosli, R., Capraro, M. M., & Capraro, R. M. (2014). The effect of science, technology, engineering and mathematics (STEM) project based learning (PBL) on students' achievement in four mathematics topics. *Journal of Turkish Science Education, 13,* 3–29.

Scherer, M. (2001). How and why standards can improve student achievement: A conversation with Robert J. Marzano. *Educational Leadership 59*(1), 14–18. Retrieved from http://www.ascd.org/publications/educational-leadership/sept01/vol59/num01/How-and-Why-Standards-Can-Improve-Student-Achievement@-A-Conversation-with-Robert-J.-Marzano.aspx

Schmidt, H. G., van der Molen, H. T., Te Winkel, W. W. R., & Wijnen, W. H. F. W. (2009). Constructivist, problem-based learning does work: A meta-analysis of curricular comparisons involving a single medical school. *Educational Psychologist, 44*(4), 227–249.

Schmoker, M. (2011). *Focus: Elevating the essentials to radically improve student learning.* Alexandria, VA: ASCD.

Schwartz, D. L., & Bransford, J. D. (1998). A time for telling. *Cognition and Instruction, 16,* 475–522. doi:10.1207/s1532690xci1604_4

Smith, R. A. (2003). *Problem-based versus lecture-based medical teaching and learning: A meta-analysis of cognitive and noncognitive outcomes* (Unpublished PhD). University of Florida, FL.

Taba, D., & Elkins, E. (1966). *Teaching strategies for the culturally disadvantaged.* Chicago, IL: Rand McNally.

Thomas, J. W. (2000). *A review of research on project-based learning. Report prepared for The Autodesk Foundation.* Retrieved from http://www.bie.org/index.php/site/RE/pbl_research/29

Tomlinson, C. A., & McTighe, J. (2006). *Integrating differentiated instruction and understanding by design: Connecting content and kids*. Alexandria, VA: ASCD.

Vernon, D. T., & Blake, R. L. (1993). Does problem-based learning work? A meta-analysis of evaluative research. *Academic Medicine, 68*(7), 550–563.

Wagner, T. (2012). *Creating innovators: The making of young people who will change the world*. New York, NY: Simon & Schuster.

Walker, A., & Leary, H. M. (2009). A problem based learning meta analysis: Differences across problem types, implementation types, disciplines, and assessment levels. *Interdisciplinary Journal of Problem Based Learning, 3*(1), 12–43.

Walker, A., & Shelton, B. E. (2008). Problem-based educational games: Connections, prescriptions, and assessment. *Journal of Interactive Learning Research, 19*(4), 663.

Way, J., & Beardon, T. (2003). *ICT and primary mathematics*. Philadelphia, PA: Open University Press.

Wiggins, G. (2013, October, 23). *Is significant school reform needed or not?: An open letter to Diane Ravitch (and like-minded educators)* [Web log post]. Retrieved from https://grantwiggins.wordpress.com/2013/10/23/is-significant-school-reform-needed-or-not-an-open-letter-to-diane-ravitch-and-like-minded-educators

Wiliam, D. (2011). *Embedded formative assessment: Practical strategies and tools for K–12 teachers*. Bloomington, IN: Solution Tree.

Wiliam, D. (2013, December). Assessment: The bridge between teaching and learning. *Voices from the Middle, 22*(2), 15–20. Retrieved from http://www.ncte.org/library/NCTEFiles/Resources/Journals/VM/0212-dec2013/VM0212Assessment.pdf

Willingham, D. (2009). *Why don't students like school?: A cognitive scientist answers questions about how the mind works and what it means for the classroom*. San Francisco, CA: Jossey-Bass.

Zeiser, K., Taylor, J., Rickles, J., Garet, M., & Segeritz, M. (2014). *Evidence of deeper learning outcomes: Findings from the Study of Deeper Learning: Opportunities and Outcomes: Report #3*. Washington, DC: American Institutes for Research.

Zhao, Y. (2012). *World class learners: Educating creative and entrepreneurial students*. Thousand Oaks, CA: Corwin.

Index

Cognitive gap, 80, 81, 98
Cognitive tension, 80
Collaborative learning, 11 (figure), 13
Competence. *See* Confident/
      competent learners
Confident/competent learners, 2–3, 5,
      9–10, 143, 144–145
   adaptive expertise, development of, 14
   assessment-capable learners and,
      11 (figure), 12–13
   attributes of, 10–13, 11 (figure)
   belief to action system and, 11, 12, 13
   collaborative learning and,
      11 (figure), 13
   deep-level learning and, 14, 15,
      15 (figure)
   effective learners, development of,
      11, 12, 13
   growth mindset and, 10–12,
      11 (figure), 13
   knowledge-based economy and, 14
   learning levels and, 14–15,
      15 (figure)
   mastery, motivation and, 12–13
   performance monitoring strategies
      and, 12–13
   social experience of learning and, 13
   strategies for learning and, 11–12
   student engagement, facilitation of, 13
   student improvement, interventions
      for, 16, 16 (figure)
   student self-reflection and, 10, 11, 12
   surface-level learning and, 14,
      14 (figure)
   teacher role and, 9–10, 11, 13,
      15–16, 16 (figure)
   transfer-level learning and, 14,
      15–16, 15 (figure)
   Visible Learning and, 9
   See also Culture of confidence design
      shift; Project-based learning design;
      Project-based learning (PBL)
Connected learning. *See* Deep/
      relational learning
Constructivist Listening feedback
   strategy, 133 (figure), 135, 139
Contexts:
   contexts of problem solving and, 6
   decontextualized learning objectives
      and, 43, 43 (figure)
   generation of, 57–58, 58 (figure)

multiple contexts and, 43–44
   similarities/differences in, xv
Corkrum, S. M., 90, 91
Critical Friends Team (CFT) feedback
   strategy, 133 (figure), 135,
   136–137, 141
Culture of confidence design shift, 28,
   31, 35, 111, 168
   agreements/protocols, all students
      learning and, 113–116,
      114–115 (figures), 130, 140
   challenging problems, solutions to,
      114, 115
   Constructivist Listening feedback
      strategy and, 133 (figure), 135, 139
   Critical Friends Team feedback
      strategy and, 133 (figure), 135,
      136–137
   culture of confidence, development
      of, 113
   deep-level learning and, 118,
      118 (figure), 119, 120–121 (figures),
      125 (figure)
   effect size considerations and,
      122–123, 127, 128 (figure)
   failure in learning, exposure to,
      130–133, 131–132 (figures)
   feedback discussions and, 129–130
   feedback processes, establishment of,
      133, 133 (figure), 135, 136–139
   growth standard, student progress/
      instructional efficacy and,
      122–124, 126–127
   intentional design of culture and,
      112–113
   know/need to know tool and, 130
   language of learning,
      establishment of, 117–119,
      118–119 (figures), 124
   learning attributes, confidence in,
      112–113
   Learning Challenge, 131 (figure)
   Learning Dilemma feedback strategy
      and, 133 (figure), 135, 138
   learning intentions and, 119, 122–124
   learning pit activities and,
      132 (figure), 133
   learning pit, cognitive disequilibrium
      and, 130, 131 (figure)
   modeling agreements/protocols
      and, 115

A SAGE Publishing Company

Helping educators make the greatest impact

CORWIN HAS ONE MISSION: to enhance education through intentional professional learning. We build long-term relationships with our authors, educators, clients, and associations who partner with us to develop and continuously improve the best evidence-based practices that establish and support lifelong learning.